The First Part of

King Henry the Fourth

Hayden Shakespeare Series

Editors:

MAYNARD MACK
Sterling Professor of English, Yale University

ROBERT W. BOYNTON
Former Principal, Senior High School,
and Chairman, English Department, Germantown Friends School

THE FIRST PART OF
KING HENRY THE FOURTH

by William Shakespeare

Edited by

Maynard Mack and Robert W. Boynton

HAYDEN BOOK COMPANY, INC., NEW YORK

The figure "The Globe Playhouse, 1599-1613, a Conjectural Reconstruction" is reprinted by permission of Coward-McCann, Inc., from *The Globe Restored: A Study of the Elizabethan Theatre*, Second Edition, by C. Walter Hodges. Copyright © 1953 and 1968 by C. Walter Hodges.

ISBN 0-8104-6017-3
Library of Congress Catalog Card Number 72-88230
Copyright © 1973
Printed in the United States of America

1	2	3	4	5	6	7	8	9	PRINTING
73	74	75	76	77	78				YEAR

PREFACE

The Hayden Shakespeare Series offers the Shakespeare plays most widely studied in schools and colleges, in a format designed to be read more easily than the normal pocket-sized editions, yet inexpensive, durable, and, more important, informed by the best in modern Shakespeare scholarship. The plays included in this series are judiciously framed with supporting material, enabling the reader to deal creatively with the text in the classroom, in small groups, or independently.

The editors of this series have founded their work on the following principles:

(1) Reading Shakespeare is not a poor substitute for seeing Shakespeare well performed, but rather a different arena of experience with its own demands and rewards.

(2) Seeing and hearing the language of the play in the theater of the mind is central to the experience the playwright provides.

(3) Knowing something of the characteristics of Shakespeare's own theater lessens the danger of asking the wrong questions about the structure and meaning of his plays.

(4) The text should be as faithful as possible to the most authoritative early edition, with a minimum of editorial interpolation.

(5) Notes and glosses should explain and not simply suggest, but at the same time the reader should be granted his common sense and his mother wit.

(6) Commentary before and after the play does not detract from direct experience—is not intrusive—if it suggests ways of approaching the text that allow the reader a broader range of imaginative involvement.

(7) Questions on the text provoke further questions and provide deepened insight if they are not used or thought of as prodding or testing devices.

Each volume in the series contains an introductory essay which briefly puts the play in its historical context (not because our interest is in theatrical history, but because the play *has* a historical context) and discusses the play's themes and concerns and how Shakespeare went about dramatizing them. Along with the introductory essay is a brief note about the Elizabethan theater, a conjectural reconstruction of the Globe Playhouse, and a general note on the policy of this series with respect to texts, with specific reference to the play in hand.

Following the text there is a commentary on how to approach the play as a live dramatic experience in the theater of the mind. Observations on the imaginative world of the play in general lead into discussions of selected scenes, the intention being to place the sometimes narrow interests of academic Shakespeare study in a context that gives scope to the whole personality of teacher and student and calls up sense and feeling as well as idea and theme.

Also included in the material following the text are questions, specific and general, on the play, some brief information about Shakespeare himself, a chronological listing of his works, and suggested basic reference books, recordings, and films.

CONTENTS

INTRODUCTION

1 Henry IV, published in 1598, probably written and acted a year or two earlier, belongs to a decade of pronounced political self-consciousness, and also political unrest, following England's great victory over the armada of Spain in 1588. Contemporary anxiety about the succession to the throne, now that Queen Elizabeth (born in 1533) was in her sixties and without an heir, may or may not have helped determine Shakespeare's choice of subject in the nine English history plays he presented during this decade, but it unquestionably gave them an extra relevance and excitement for their first audiences. Some men were yet alive who could remember the troubles that threatened the succession on the death of Elizabeth's father, Henry VIII. Almost everyone had heard, through the chronicles of Holinshed and his like (Shakespeare's own sources) or through legend and hearsay, of the anarchy that ensued on the death of Henry V (the subject of Shakespeare's earlier tetralogy); and, again before that, on the deposition and death of Richard II, brought about by his successor, the Henry IV of our play. London gossip in the 1590's sometimes hinted darkly that similar eventualities awaited the aging Queen. When in 1601 her favorite, the Earl of Essex, did make an abortive attempt to invade her power, Shakespeare's play about Richard's deposition and murder was performed, we must suppose significantly, at Essex House the night before.

Shakespeare's usurper in *1 Henry IV* is a man who by his personal combination of sagacity and cunning, prudence and force, is far better equipped to be a king than was his predecessor, whose unflattering portrait he paints with some relish when

I

lecturing his son on the responsibilities of princes in III ii
60-73:

> The skipping King, he ambled up and down
> With shallow jesters and rash bavin wits,
> Soon kindled and soon burnt; carded his state;
> Mingled his royalty with cap'ring fools;
> Had his great name profanèd with their scorns
> And gave his countenance, against his name,
> To laugh at gibing boys and stand the push
> Of every beardless vain comparative;
> Grew a companion to the common streets,
> Enfeoffed himself to popularity;
> That, being daily swallowed by men's eyes,
> They surfeited with honey and began
> To loathe the taste of sweetness, whereof a little
> More than a little is by much too much.

Richard had been irresponsible and self-indulgent without question—at least as presented by Henry here, and by Shakespeare,
drawing on Tudor historians, in the earlier play. On the other
hand, Richard's right to occupy the throne of which Henry had
deprived him was indisputable, and Henry's act in deposing him,
much more in causing him to be murdered, was a grave wrong
(in religious terms, a sin), which could be counted on to bring
retribution not only on himself, but on the entire English people in time to come. In the main, the nation had been on Henry's
side when he returned from the exile abroad to which Richard
had condemned him, seeking to retrieve by armed force if necessary the lands due him from his father which Richard had
seized. And when unforeseen events pushed Henry toward and
finally onto the throne, most of the nation had continued to go
along, especially the Percy family, though as they look back on
it now, the Percys are inclined to think they did not really intend
this result and have therefore decided to use the uncertainty of
Henry's title to the throne as justification for a new revolt. All
this had been foretold by Richard as he was led off to prison
and death in the earlier play, addressing the very man whom
we meet again in this play:

> Northumberland, thou ladder wherewithal
> The mounting Bolingbroke ascends my throne,
> The time shall not be many hours of age
> More than it is, ere foul sin, gathering head,

Shall break into corruption. Thou shalt think,
Though he divide the realm and give thee half,
It is too little, helping him to all;
He shall think that thou which knowest the way
To plant unrightful kings, wilt know again,
Being ne'er so little urged another way,
To pluck him headlong from the usurped throne.
The love of wicked men converts to fear,
That fear to hate, and hate turns one or both
To worthy danger and deservèd death.

(V i 55-68)

The political vein in *1 Henry IV* consists largely in the working out of this prediction.

The play's comic vein, though it is exuberant and joyous in its own right, is designed to comment shrewdly on the political themes. The lawlessness of Falstaff and his crew, with a crown prince participating, reflects in an oblique way a pervasive lawlessness infecting the whole realm—expressed equally in Henry's own act in seizing the throne from Richard and in the rebels' attempt now to seize it back from Henry. England, like the inn at Rochester (II i), has become a place of disorder and decay ("since Robin Ostler died"), where every man is rightly suspicious of his fellow. Fat, drunken, lazy, cowardly, and generally irresponsible—but also witty, affectionate, and frankly unpolitical, with a withering scorn for all forms of pomposity and pretension (witness his parodies of the Puritans and the Court)—Falstaff is representative of what ails Henry's England in two ways. On the one hand, he embodies the unruliness that the Prince must learn to put away before he can make a good king. On the other hand, he embodies a breadth of humanity, an acknowledgment of frailty, that the King too much lacks and that the Prince will be the better for taking with him when he ascends his father's throne.

Hotspur is in many ways Falstaff's alter ego, despite the immense differences between them at first sight. Each is conscious of the claims of the chivalric code of honor, Falstaff to puncture them ("Honor is a mere scutcheon"), Hotspur to blow them up romantically in a highly colored but inaccessible balloon ("By heaven, methinks it were an easy leap/To pluck bright honor from the pale-faced moon"). Each seeks to conceal from himself harsh truths, Falstaff constantly adjusting the realities of Hal's future reign so as to leave a niche for himself ("By the Lord, I'll be a brave judge"), Hotspur refusing repeatedly to accept the evidence borne in on him from all quarters that the rebellion is doomed. Though Falstaff is only thirsty, Hotspur bloodthirsty, each leads his troops into battle with a sublime unconcern for any interests but his own. Hotspur is impatient with Glendower, Falstaff with Mistress Quickly; Hotspur takes Mortimer's and Worcester's reproof with ill grace; Falstaff does likewise with Bardolph's; Hotspur closes II iii chattering about his horse, Falstaff opens II ii bawling for his; Hotspur imagines an epic battle between Mortimer and Glendower, Falstaff imagines a yet more epic encounter between himself and eleven men in buckram. In scene after scene, incident after incident, Shakespeare poses these two figures against and alongside each other, so that by the play's end we may see clearly how much Hal has distinguished himself from them while at the same time incorporating in himself the best each has to offer. They are the extremes between which his path must lead if he is to be a great king; and when at the climax of the battle he towers over both—Hotspur now dead and Falstaff playing dead—it is brought home to us in an unforgettably visual way that to Henry's victory in the struggle against the rebels must be added Hal's victory in a far larger sphere.

A Note on the Elizabethan Theater

Most present-day productions of Elizabethan plays use sets designed to provide a single flexible and suggestive background against which their multiple scenes can flow easily one into the next. Elizabethan plays have to be staged that way if they are not to be distorted, because that is the way they are built. Though the modern playwright is limited by the nature of his theater to as few changes of locale as possible, his Elizabethan counterpart was encouraged by *his* theater to range the whole world of space and time, because his theater was in fact an image of the world. Shakespeare's own theater was even called the world—i.e., the "Globe."

In today's theaters, for the most part, audience and play are emphatically separate. They are separated physically by the architecture of the theater, which has a drop-curtain, footlights, often an orchestra pit, and always a proscenium arch (the arch covered by the curtain), on one side of which the audience sits hushed in almost total darkness, while on the other side the persons of the play move and talk in spots, or floods, of blazing light.

This physical separation of audience from play is expressive of the figurative gulf which, in our theater, also divides them. For the illusion that the modern theater imposes is that the audience is "not really" present, but is eavesdropping, and that the people it looks in on are "really" men and women going about real business in a real room from which one wall has been removed.

What this means for those on the bright side of the footlights is that everything must be made as completely "present" as actors, scene-painters, and stage-carpenters can manage; it is not enough to suggest reality, it must be simulated. The implication for those on the dark side of the footlights is that they must become as "unpresent" as they can—in other words detached, silent, and passive, like the eavesdroppers they are. Actually, neither of these extremes is ever reached in our theater, or even closely approached, but the tendency of enhanced realism on one side of the curtain to generate passivity on the other has spurred many modern playwrights to search for ways of recapturing the cooperative relation between audience and play that Shakespeare's theater had.

Physically the Globe was a wooden building shaped probably like a polygon outside and circular inside, some thirty or forty feet high, with three tiers of roofed galleries, one on top of the other straight up, opera-house style, around the entire interior. The center of the enclosure (the "pit"), some fifty or so feet in diameter, was unroofed, and into it jutted the raised rectangular stage, fully half the way across the pit and almost forty feet wide. Above part of the stage, as a cover, supported on pillars, was a sloping roof, called the "Heavens," the ceiling of which was brightly painted with stars and other astronomical figures. Below the stage, reached by trap doors, was "Hell." At the rear

THE GLOBE PLAYHOUSE, 1599–1613

A Conjectural Reconstruction

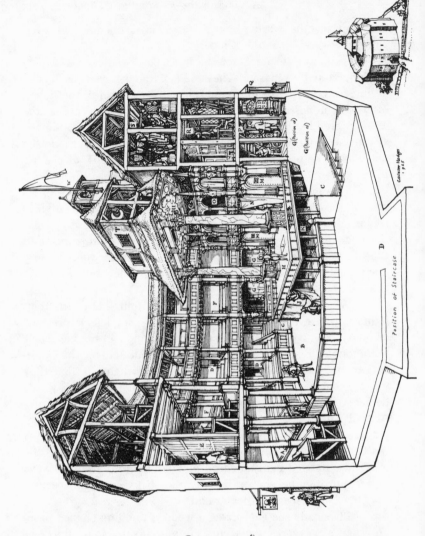

Key

AA   Main entrance
B   The Yard
CC   Entrances to lowest gallery
D   Entrances to staircase and upper
     galleries
E   Corridor serving the different
     sections of the middle gallery
F   Middle gallery ("Twopenny Rooms")
G   "Gentlemen's Rooms" or "Lords'
     Rooms"
H   The stage
J   The hanging being put up around
     the stage
K   The "Hell" under the stage
L   The stage trap, leading down to the
     "Hell"
MM   Stage doors
N   Curtained "place behind the stage"
O   Gallery above the stage, used as
     required—sometimes by
     musicians, sometimes by
     spectators, and often as part
     of the play
P   Backstage area (the tiring-house)
Q   Tiring-house door
R   Dressing rooms
S   Wardrobe and storage
T   The hut housing the machine for
     lowering enthroned gods, etc.,
     to the stage
U   The "Heavens"
W   Hoisting the playhouse flag

wall, doors on either side gave access between the stage and the dressing rooms. Toward the rear of the stage there was an "inner" playing area, probably a sort of alcove (but sometimes misleadingly called the "inner stage"), which could be left opened or curtained. Directly above this was an "upper" playing area (the "upper stage"), which probably took the form of a balcony. Above this was another, smaller balcony for the musicians; for the use of music, in tragedy as well as comedy, was one of the conventions of Elizabethan plays.

What scenery there was in theaters like the Globe took chiefly the form of simple props. There was no artificial lighting of any kind in the theater, which meant that performances were always given by daylight—in the afternoon. The interior of the building was handsomely decorated, and the dress of the actors (males only—boys played the female roles) expensive and resplendent, although there was little concern for what we would call authentic period costuming.

The important thing to bear in mind about the Elizabethan theater is that the stage physically dominated the open area and that the audience literally enveloped the actors and the action. As many as two thousand people might be present. Many stood shoulder to shoulder in the pit, surrounding the chest-high open platform on three sides. Behind them in the tiered galleries, at no place more than forty or fifty feet from the stage, sat hundreds of others on benches. In these circumstances, it was easy for the viewers' sense of involvement in the play, and the actors' sense of involvement with the audience before and behind them, to become more intense than in our theater.

The playwright who writes for such a theater as this cannot shape his play as if the audience were not "there": it is irremovably there, every member of it visible to every other in the broad light coming from the open roof. So he necessarily acknowledges its presence, engages its imagination. He feels free, for example, to give his characters "asides"—speeches spoken wholly or mainly for the benefit of the audience, and which those on stage are not supposed to hear. He also gives his characters "soliloquies"—longer speeches by means of which the leading characters may open heart and mind directly to the audience. Further, since his stage is a bare platform without scenery, he calls repeatedly on the imagination of the audience to flesh out the suggestions of hour, place, weather, or mood that he can only communicate to them through the play's own words.

The dramatist who writes for the theater we have been describing has unparalleled opportunities to make the theater audience do duty as an extension, an overflow, an amplification of the very limited stage-audiences which a small company of actors can muster. When, for instance, Shakespeare's Antony addresses the Roman mob in *Julius Caesar*, in a theater where we of the audience surround him on three sides, the realization comes on us increasingly as he speaks that it is we who fill out that tiny group of listeners onstage into the formidable mob he *seems* to harangue; and when King Harry in *Henry V* exhorts his soldiers—"You noblest English"—to battle bravely against the French, we realize (as Shakespeare's own audiences must have done, and in their case with a sharp quickening of the pulse) that it is *we* who are being addressed: *we* are those "noblest English" who are being implored never to yield.

Interactions like these between play and audience are not impossible in the modern theater, but they were a good deal easier to effect in Shakespeare's. Partly, as we have noticed, because of the close physical proximity of audience to player. Partly, as we have also noticed, because the audience's imagination was implicated in the play by the very austerity of a stage without scenery. And partly because the Elizabethan theater's inheritance from the medieval theater (where the stories acted out were primarily Bible stories and therefore "true" in one sense while remaining "stories" in another sense) encouraged an easy traffic back and forth between what was "real" and what was "play."

As has been mentioned, over part of the stage stretched a ceiling called the "Heavens," and under the stage, reached by trap doors through which witches and other apparitions might rise, lay an area called "Hell." And in front of the theater, in the case of Shakespeare's Globe (if we may believe a plausible tradition), was inscribed the legend: *Totus mundus agit histrionem*—"Everybody is an actor"; or, as Shakespeare himself paraphrased it in *As You Like It*, "All the world's a stage, and all the men and women merely players." Thus the individual actor whom the audience saw on the stage playing Julius Caesar or Hamlet or Macbeth was capable of being translated, at any moment, by the very symbolism of that stage, into an image of Every Man working out his human destiny (as the men and women watching him would also have to work out theirs) between the powers of Hell and Heaven.

It is because the characters of Shakespeare were created for a theater like this that they take special hold of us. They have the intensity that comes from believing that the world is a stage, where we are given only our little hour to work out eternal salvation or damnation: and they have the grandeur that comes from believing that the stage is a world, which reaches out past the actors to the theater audience, past them to the audience we call history, past this to the cosmic audience of land, sea, air, moon, sun, and stars (which Elizabethan heroes do not hesitate to address), and so at last to the audience Hamlet turns to when the appearance of the Ghost makes it unmistakable that there are more things in heaven and earth than are dreamed of in human philosophies: "Angels and ministers of grace defend us!"

Textual Note

Although Shakespeare had no connection with their actual publication, eighteen of his thirty-seven plays were published in various quarto editions before his death in 1616. Not until 1623 were all but one of the plays usually credited to him published in a single volume, now called the First Folio. (A folio is a book made up of sheets folded in half, creating four individual pages per sheet; a quarto is one made up of sheets folded in half and in half again, producing eight pages per sheet.) The First Folio was compiled by two of Shakespeare's actor-colleagues who drew upon the best previous quarto editions of single plays, where available, and on fairly reliable unpublished manuscripts and theater promptbooks. For whatever reason, they omitted from their collection two plays which most scholars today attribute wholly or in part to Shakespeare (*Pericles, Prince of Tyre* and *The Two Noble Kinsmen*) and one play (*Sir Thomas More*) in which it is believed he had a hand.

The policy of the Hayden Shakespeare Series is to use the earliest sound version of each play—either the Folio text or (if one exists) a good quarto text with collations from the Folio—and a minimum of emendation. In lineation, we follow a similarly conservative policy. Most modern editors space the line fragments, with which two successive speeches often end and begin, as a single pentameter line. A case can be made for this procedure, but after considerable reflection we have abandoned it, because we believe that in these situations the lineation of the original editions more often than not throws interesting light on speaking emphasis, pause, and rhythm, and also eliminates a possible reading distraction. We have everywhere normalized and modernized the spelling and punctuation of the original texts, printed character names in full, and added (inconspicuously) act-scene divisions, following the practice of the Globe edition (1864), to which concordances of Shakespeare refer. All matter placed in brackets in the text, including stage directions, is editorial and does not appear in the original version being used.

The line numbering and the act-scene indicators at the top of each page are for convenient reference. The small degree sign (°) indicates a gloss or footnote at the bottom of the page, keyed by line number. The cue phrase is printed in boldface, the gloss or footnote in roman.

The text for *1 Henry IV* is primarily the first quarto of 1598, generally believed to have been set from an earlier edition of the same year (Q0), of which only four leaves are known —containing the text of the play from I iii 199 to II ii 112. Q0, so far as we have it, shows characteristics which relate it to an authorial manuscript, probably a corrected working manuscript. Q1 may therefore be regarded as still reasonably faithful to what Shakespeare wrote. The later quartos (Q2, 1599; Q3, 1604; Q4, 1608; Q5, 1613), each set from the preceding, and the First Folio, set from Q5, have increasingly less authority. We have followed Q1, and, where it exists, Q0. With one exception (IV i 12-13) we preserve the lineation of these editions, printing as prose a number of passages so printed in Q1, but now almost invariably divided (impressionistically!) into lines of verse.

THE FIRST PART OF

KING HENRY THE FOURTH

[Dramatis Personae

KING HENRY THE FOURTH
HENRY, Prince of Wales ⎫
PRINCE JOHN of Lancaster ⎰ the King's sons
EARL OF WESTMORELAND
SIR WALTER BLUNT
THOMAS PERCY, Earl of Worcester
HENRY PERCY, Earl of Northumberland
HENRY PERCY ("Hotspur"), his son
EDMUND MORTIMER, Earl of March
RICHARD SCROOP, Archbishop of York
ARCHIBALD, Earl of Douglas
OWEN GLENDOWER
SIR RICHARD VERNON
SIR JOHN FALSTAFF
SIR MICHAEL, a friend of the Archbishop of York
POINS
GADSHILL
PETO
BARDOLPH
FRANCIS, a waiter
LADY PERCY, Hotspur's wife and Mortimer's sister
LADY MORTIMER, Glendower's daughter and Mortimer's wife
MISTRESS QUICKLY, hostess of the tavern
SHERIFF, VINTNER, CHAMBERLAIN, TWO CARRIERS, OSTLER,
    MESSENGERS, TRAVELERS, ATTENDANTS

Scene: England and Wales]

THE FIRST PART OF

KING HENRY THE FOURTH

I i

Enter the King, Lord John of Lancaster, Earl of
Westmoreland, [Sir Walter Blunt,] with others.

KING.   So shaken° as we are, so wan with care,
Find we° a time for frighted peace to pant°
And breathe short-winded accents of new broils°
To be commenced in stronds° afar remote.
No more the thirsty entrance of this soil   5
Shall daub her lips with her own children's blood,
No more shall trenching° war channel her fields,
Nor bruise her flow'rets with the armèd hoofs
Of hostile paces. Those opposèd eyes
Which, like the meteors° of a troubled heaven,   10
All of one nature, of one substance bred,°
Did lately meet in the intestine° shock
And furious close° of civil butchery,
Shall now in mutual well-beseeming° ranks
March all one way and be no more opposed   15
Against acquaintance, kindred, and allies.
The edge of war, like an ill-sheathèd knife,
No more shall cut his master. Therefore, friends,
As far as to the sepulcher of Christ°—
Whose soldier now, under whose blessèd cross   20

I i 1   **shaken**   i.e. by civil wars
2   **Find we**   let us find
2   **pant**   catch (her) breath
3   **broils**   battles
4   **stronds**   strands, i.e. shores
7   **trenching**   (1) cutting   (2) encroaching
10   **meteors**   atmospheric disturbances
11   **All . . . bred**   i.e. because believed to originate from vapors
12   **intestine**   internal
13   **close**   grappling
14   **well-beseeming**   orderly
19   **As . . . Christ**   i.e. to Jerusalem

We are impressèd and engaged° to fight—
Forthwith a power° of English shall we levy,
Whose arms were molded in their mother's womb
To chase these pagans in those holy fields
Over whose acres walked those blessèd feet   25
Which fourteen hundred years ago were nailed
For our advantage on the bitter cross.
But this our purpose now is twelvemonth old,
And bootless° 'tis to tell you we will go.
Therefor we meet not now.° Then let me hear   30
Of you, my gentle cousin° Westmoreland,
What yesternight our council did decree°
In forwarding this dear expedience.°

WESTMORELAND.   My liege, this haste was hot in question°
And many limits of the charge° set down   35
But yesternight; when all athwart° there came
A post° from Wales, loaden with heavy news,
Whose worst was that the noble Mortimer,
Leading the men of Herefordshire to fight
Against the irregular and wild° Glendower,   40
Was by the rude hands of that Welshman taken,
A thousand of his people butcherèd;
Upon whose dead corpse° there was such misuse,
Such beastly shameless transformation
By those Welshwomen done, as may not be   45
Without much shame retold or spoken of.°

KING.   It seems then that the tidings of this broil
Brake° off our business for the Holy Land.

WESTMORELAND.   This, matched with other, did, my gracious
          lord;
For more uneven° and unwelcome news   50
Came from the north, and thus it did import:

---

21 **impressèd and engaged** conscripted
and pledged (i.e. by Henry's vow to do
penance for the murder of Richard: see
Richard II, V v 45-50)
22 **power** army
29 **bootless** useless
30 **Therefor . . . now** that is not the reason we meet now
31 **gentle cousin** noble kinsman
32 **decree** decide
33 **dear expedience** desired undertaking
34 **hot in question** hotly debated

35 **limits . . . charge** assigning of duties
and costs
36 **athwart** cutting across, i.e. interfering
37 **post** messenger
40 **irregular and wild** i.e. as a border-
raider and guerrilla
43 **corpse** corpses
44-46 **Such . . . spoken of** (the phrasing
in Holinshed, Shakespeare's source, suggests
that the dead English were castrated)
48 **Brake** broke
50 **uneven** (see "smooth," line 66)

On Holy-rood Day° the gallant Hotspur there,
Young Harry Percy, and brave Archibald,
That ever-valiant and approvèd° Scot
At Holmedon° met, where they did spend   55
A sad and bloody hour;
As by discharge of their artillery
And shape of likelihood° the news was told;
For he that brought them,° in the very heat
And pride of their contention° did take horse,   60
Uncertain of the issue° any way.

KING.   Here is a dear, a true industrious° friend,
Sir Walter Blunt, new lighted from his horse,
Stained with the variation of each soil
Betwixt that Holmedon and this seat° of ours,   65
And he hath brought us smooth and welcome news.
The Earl of Douglas is discomfited;°
Ten thousand bold Scots, two and twenty knights,
Balked° in their own blood did Sir Walter see
On Holmedon's plains. Of prisoners, Hotspur took   70
Mordake, Earl of Fife and eldest son
To beaten Douglas, and the Earl of Athol,
Of Murray, Angus, and Menteith.
And is not this an honorable spoil?
A gallant prize? Ha, cousin, is it not?   75

WESTMORELAND.   In faith° it is. A conquest for a prince to
boast of.

KING.   Yea, there thou mak'st me sad, and mak'st me sin
In envy that my Lord Northumberland
Should be the father to so blest a son:
A son who is the theme of honor's tongue,   80
Amongst a grove the very straightest plant;
Who is sweet fortune's minion° and her pride;
Whilst I, by looking on the praise of him,
See riot and dishonor stain the brow

---

52 **Holy-rood Day** September 14
54 **approvèd** of tested bravery
55 **Holmedon** Humbleton in Northumberland
58 **shape of likelihood** probability
59 **them** i.e. the news
59-60 **heat . . . contention** peak of battle

61 **issue** outcome
62 **true industrious** loyally zealous
65 **seat** dwelling, i.e. the palace
67 **discomfited** routed
69 **Balked** (1) heaped (2) thwarted
76 **In faith** truly
82 **minion** darling

Of my young Harry. O that it could be proved   85
That some night-tripping fairy° had exchanged
In cradle clothes our children where they lay,
And called mine Percy, his Plantagenet!°
Then would I have his Harry, and he mine.
But let him° from my thoughts. What think you, coz,°   90
Of this young Percy's pride?° The prisoners
Which he in this adventure hath surprised°
To his own use he keeps, and sends me word
I shall have none but Mordake, Earl of Fife.

WESTMORELAND.   This is his uncle's teaching, this is Worcester, 95
Malevolent to you in all aspects,°
Which makes him prune° himself and bristle up
The crest of youth against your dignity.°

KING.   But I have sent for him to answer this;
And for this cause awhile we must neglect   100
Our holy purpose to Jerusalem.
Cousin, on Wednesday next our council we
Will hold at Windsor, so inform the lords:
But come yourself with speed to us again,
For more is to be said and to be done   105
Than out of anger can be utterèd.°

WESTMORELAND.   I will, my liege.   *Exeunt.*

∽◦◦◦∽

Enter Prince of Wales and Sir John Falstaff.   *I ii*

FALSTAFF.   Now, Hal, what time of day is it, lad?

PRINCE.   Thou art so fat-witted with drinking of old sack,° and
unbuttoning thee after supper, and sleeping upon benches
after noon, that thou hast forgotten to demand that truly

---

86 **fairy** (fairies were said to substitute an
ugly "changeling" for a beautiful child)
88 **Plantagenet** family name of Henry IV
90 **let him** let me dismiss him
90 **coz** kinsman (short for "cousin")
91 **pride** presumption
92 **surprised** taken

96 **Malevolent . . . aspects** (an astrological
expression comparing Worcester to a planet
whose influence obstructs Henry's designs)
97 **prune** preen his feathers for action
(like a hawk)
98 **dignity** authority
106 **utterèd** publicly discussed
I ii 2 **sack** Spanish white wine

which thou wouldest truly know. What a devil hast thou to   5
do with the time of the day? Unless hours were cups of
sack, and minutes capons, and clocks the tongues of bawds,°
and dials° the signs of leaping houses,° and the blessed sun
himself a fair hot wench in flame-colored taffeta, I see no
reason why thou shouldst be so superfluous to° demand the   10
time of the day.

FALSTAFF.   Indeed you come near me° now, Hal; for we that
take purses go by° the moon and the seven stars,° and not
by Phoebus,° he, that wand'ring knight so fair.° And I
prithee, sweet wag,° when thou art a king, as, God save thy   15
Grace°—Majesty I should say, for grace thou wilt have
none—

PRINCE.   What, none?

FALSTAFF.   No, by my troth;° not so much as will serve to be
prologue to an egg and butter.°   20

PRINCE.   Well, how then? Come, roundly, roundly.°

FALSTAFF.   Marry,° then, sweet wag, when thou art king, let
not us that are squires of the night's body be called thieves
of the day's beauty.° Let us be Diana's° foresters, gentlemen of the shade, minions° of the moon; and let men say   25
we be men of good government,° being governed, as the
sea is, by our noble and chaste mistress the moon, under
whose countenance we steal.

---

7 bawds brothel-keepers
8 dials sundials
8 leaping houses brothels
10 so . . . to so irrelevant as to
12 near me i.e. close to understanding
me (as if Hal were shooting at a mark)
13 go by (1) walk under (2) tell time by
(3) regulate our lives by
13 seven stars constellation Pleiades
14 Phoebus the sun
14 he . . . fair (Falstaff possibly quotes
here, or sings, a line of a lost ballad; the
sun was readily thought of as an eternal
wanderer or "knight-errant")
15 wag mischief-maker
16 Grace (Falstaff puns on "your Grace"—
a title which Hal as king will exchange for
"your Majesty"—and spiritual grace, and, in
lines 19-20, on grace before eating)
19 troth faith
20 prologue . . . butter i.e. a (small)
grace before a small meal
21 roundly i.e. get to the point (but possibly with a glance at Falstaff's girth)

22 Marry (a mild oath, from "By the Vir-
gin Mary")
23-24 squires . . . beauty (Falstaff puns on
"night/knight"—knights were often attended
by body-squires—and probably on "body/
beauty/booty"; the "day's beauty" in one
of its senses here is the sun and balances
"the night's body," which in one sense is
the moon)
24 Diana goddess of the moon and the
hunt (by identifying the hunt with hunting
for "booty"—and "beauty"—Falstaff presents himself and his crew as Diana's companion foresters, her titled "Gentlemen of
the Shade," her "minions," who "steal"—
i.e. (1) move silently (2) take purses under
her "countenance"—i.e. under (1) her face
(2) her protection)
25 minions servants and favorites
26 of . . . government (1) well-behaved
(2) ruled by a good ruler

PRINCE. Thou sayest well, and it holds well° too; for the fortune
of us that are the moon's men doth ebb and flow like the   30
sea, being governed as the sea is by the moon. As, for proof
now: a purse of gold most resolutely snatched on Monday
night and most dissolutely spent on Tuesday morning; got
with swearing "Lay by," and spent with crying "Bring in";°
now in as low an ebb as the foot of the ladder,° and by   35
and by in as high a flow as the ridge of the gallows.

FALSTAFF. By the Lord, thou say'st true, lad—and is not my
hostess of the tavern° a most sweet wench?

PRINCE. As the honey of Hybla,° my old lad of the castle°—
and is not a buff jerkin a most sweet robe of durance?°   40

FALSTAFF. How now, how now, mad wag? What, in thy quips
and thy quiddities?° What a plague have I to do with a buff
jerkin?

PRINCE. Why, what a pox° have I to do with my hostess of the
tavern?   45

FALSTAFF. Well, thou hast called her to a reckoning° many a
time and oft.

PRINCE. Did I ever call for thee to pay thy part?

FALSTAFF. No; I'll give thee thy due, thou hast paid all there.

PRINCE. Yea, and elsewhere, so far as my coin would stretch;   50
and where it would not, I have used my credit.

FALSTAFF. Yea, and so used it that, were it not here apparent
that thou art heir apparent—But I prithee, sweet wag, shall
there be gallows standing in England when thou art king?
And resolution thus fubbed° as it is with the rusty curb of   55
old father Antic° the law? Do not thou, when thou art king,
hang a thief.

---

29 **it . . . well** it's an appropriate comparison
34 **Lay by . . . Bring in** (the highwayman's
commands: the first to his victims, the second to the waiter in the tavern where he
spends his gains)
35 **ladder** (leading up to the gallows)
38 **hostess . . . tavern** i.e. Mistress Quickly, who first appears in II iv
39 **Hybla** in Sicily, famous for its sweet
honey
39 **old . . . castle** old roisterer (with pun
on "Oldcastle," Falstaff's name in the play's
first performances, and probably on "The
Castle," a well-known London brothel)

40 **buff . . . durance** tan leather jacket—
a "robe of durance" because both "durable" and symbolically "confining" (it was
the costume of the sheriff's officers)
42 **quiddities** witty word games
44 **pox** (the Prince turns Falstaff's "plague"
into a disease more characteristic of tavern
hostesses)
46 **called . . . reckoning** (1) called her to
a showdown (2) asked her for the bill
55 **resolution . . . fubbed** courage (i.e. in
the highwayman) thus cheated of its reward
56 **old . . . Antic** i.e. "that old screwball"

PRINCE. No; thou shalt.

FALSTAFF. Shall I? O rare! By the Lord, I'll be a brave° judge.

PRINCE. Thou judgest false already. I mean, thou shalt have 60
the hanging of the thieves and so become a rare hangman.

FALSTAFF. Well, Hal, well; and in some sort it jumps with my
humor° as well as waiting in the court, I can tell you.

PRINCE. For obtaining of suits?°

FALSTAFF. Yea, for obtaining of suits, whereof the hangman 65
hath no lean wardrobe. 'Sblood,° I am as melancholy as a
gib-cat° or a lugged° bear.

PRINCE. Or an old lion, or a lover's lute.

FALSTAFF. Yea, or the drone° of a Lincolnshire bagpipe.

PRINCE. What sayest thou to a hare,° or the melancholy of 70
Moorditch?°

FALSTAFF. Thou hast the most unsavory similes, and art
indeed the most comparative,° rascalliest, sweet young
prince. But, Hal, I prithee trouble me no more with vanity.°
I would to God thou and I knew where a commodity° of 75
good names were to be bought. An old lord of the council
rated° me the other day in the street about you, sir, but I
marked him not;° and yet he talked very wisely, but I
regarded him not; and yet he talked wisely, and in the
street too.   80

PRINCE. Thou didst well, for wisdom cries out in the streets,
and no man regards it.°

FALSTAFF. O, thou hast damnable iteration,° and art indeed
able to corrupt a saint. Thou hast done much harm upon

---

59 brave (1) excellent (2) handsomely at-
tired
62-63 jumps . . . humor agrees with my
frame of mind
64 suits petitions for court favor (but Falstaff takes it in the sense of the victim's
garments, which were forfeit to the execu-
tioner)
66 'Sblood by God's (i.e. Christ's) blood
67 gib-cat tomcat
67 lugged i.e. tied to a stake and baited
by dogs, as entertainment
69 drone single note of a bagpipe's bass
pipe
70 hare (proverbially melancholy)
71 Moorditch foul London drainage ditch
73 comparative full of (insulting) comparisons

74 vanity i.e. worldly considerations (Falstaff here takes up one of his favorite humorous roles, assuming for the next several
lines the sanctimonious attitudes and vocab-
ulary of Elizabethan Puritanism)
75 commodity supply
77 rated scolded
78 marked . . . not paid him no attention
81-82 Thou . . . it (Hal quotes Proverbs
1:20-24: "Wisdom crieth without, and put-
teth forth her voice in the streets . . . saying . . . 'I have stretched out my hand, and
no man regarded' ")
83 damnable iteration i.e. a sinful way of
repeating and (mis)applying holy texts

me, Hal—God forgive thee for it! Before I knew thee, Hal, 85
I knew nothing; and now am I, if a man should speak
truly, little better than one of the wicked.° I must give
over° this life, and I will give it over! By the Lord, and°
I do not, I am a villain! I'll be damned for never a king's
son in Christendom.   90

PRINCE.   Where shall we take a purse tomorrow, Jack?

FALSTAFF.   Zounds,° where thou wilt, lad! I'll make one.° An°
I do not, call me villain and baffle° me.

PRINCE.   I see a good amendment° of life in thee—from praying to purse-taking.   95

FALSTAFF.   Why, Hal, 'tis my vocation,° Hal. 'Tis no sin for a
man to labor in his vocation.

Enter Poins.

Poins! Now shall we know if Gadshill° have set a match.°
O, if men were to be saved by merit,° what hole in hell
were hot enough for him? This is the most omnipotent° 100
villain that ever cried "Stand!" to a true° man.

PRINCE.   Good morrow, Ned.

POINS.   Good morrow, sweet Hal. What says Monsieur Remorse?° What says Sir John Sack and Sugar?° Jack, how
agrees the devil and thee about thy soul, that thou soldest 105
him on Good Friday last for a cup of Madeira° and a cold
capon's leg?

PRINCE.   Sir John stands to° his word, the devil shall have his
bargain; for he was never yet a breaker of proverbs. He
will give the devil his due.   110

---

87 the wicked (Puritan idiom for those who were not Puritans; see "saint" in line 84, which glances at the Puritans' way of referring collectively to themselves)
87-88 give over give up
88 and if
92 Zounds by God's (i.e. Christ's) wounds
92 one i.e. one of the group
92 An if
93 baffle hang upside down (a punishment allotted perjured knights)
94 amendment improvement
96 vocation calling (with reference to the Puritan stress on a man's being "called" by God to his work)
98 Gadshill one of the gang of robbers (not to be confused with Gad's Hill in line 115)

98 set a match (thieves' jargon for setting up a robbery by getting information about a possible victim)
99 merit i.e. good works (in Puritan doctrine wholly insufficient for salvation)
100 omnipotent thoroughgoing
101 true honest
103-4 What . . . Remorse (addressed to Falstaff in allusion to his habit of [mock] repentance—see III iii)
104 Sack and Sugar (sack sweetened with sugar was particularly the drink of the elderly, but there may be a pun, in this context, on sackcloth and ashes, symbols of penance)
106 Madeira a sweet white wine
108 stands to is true to

POINS.   Then art thou damned for keeping thy word with the
devil.

PRINCE.   Else he had been damned for cozening° the devil.

POINS.   But, my lads, my lads, tomorrow morning, by four
o'clock early, at Gad's Hill!° There are pilgrims going to   115
Canterbury with rich offerings,° and traders riding to
London with fat purses. I have vizards° for you all; you
have horses for yourselves. Gadshill lies° tonight in
Rochester. I have bespoke° supper tomorrow night in Eastcheap.° We may do it as secure as sleep. If you will go,   120
I will stuff your purses full of crowns;° if you will not,
tarry at home and be hanged!

FALSTAFF.   Hear ye, Yedward:° if I tarry at home and go not,
I'll hang you for going.

POINS.   You will, chops?°   125

FALSTAFF.   Hal, wilt thou make one?

PRINCE.   Who, I rob? I a thief? Not I, by my faith.

FALSTAFF.   There's neither honesty, manhood, nor good fellowship in thee, nor thou cam'st not of the blood royal° if thou
darest not stand for° ten shillings.   130

PRINCE.   Well then, once in my days I'll be a madcap.

FALSTAFF.   Why, that's well said.

PRINCE.   Well, come what will, I'll tarry at home.

FALSTAFF.   By the Lord, I'll be a traitor then, when thou art
king.   135

PRINCE.   I care not.

POINS.   Sir John, I prithee, leave the Prince and me alone. I
will lay him down° such reasons for this adventure that
he shall go.

---

113 **cozening** cheating
115 **Gad's Hill** a place notorious for high-
way robberies, near Rochester, on the road
between Canterbury and London
116 **offerings** i.e. for the shrine of St.
Thomas à Becket
117 **vizards** masks
118 **lies** lodges
119 **bespoke** arranged for
119-20 **Eastcheap** London street and district

121 **crowns** coins (stamped with the royal
crown)
123 **Yedward** (dialect form of Edward)
125 **chops** "fat-face"
129 **royal** (pun on "royal," a ten-shilling
coin)
130 **stand for** (1) pass for (as a coin) (2)
contest for (in a robbery)
138 **lay him down** give him

FALSTAFF.   Well, God give thee the spirit of persuasion and   140
him the ears of profiting, that what thou speakest may
move° and what he hears may be believed, that the true
prince may (for recreation sake) prove a false thief; for
the poor abuses of the time want countenance.° Farewell;
you shall find me in Eastcheap.   145

PRINCE.   Farewell, the° latter spring! Farewell, All-hallow
summer!°   [*Exit Falstaff.*]

POINS.   Now, my good sweet honey lord, ride with us tomorrow.
I have a jest to execute that I cannot manage alone.
Falstaff, Bardolph, Peto, and Gadshill shall rob those men   150
that we have already waylaid;° yourself and I will not be
there; and when they have the booty, if you and I do not
rob them, cut this head off from my shoulders.

PRINCE.   How shall we part with them in setting forth?

POINS.   Why, we will set forth before or after them and ap-   155
point them a place of meeting, wherein it is at our pleasure
to fail; and then will they adventure upon° the exploit
themselves, which they shall have no sooner achieved, but
we'll set upon them.

PRINCE.   Yea, but 'tis like that they will know us by our horses,   160
by our habits,° and by every other appointment,° to be
ourselves.

POINS.   Tut! Our horses they shall not see—I'll tie them in the
wood; our vizards we will change after we leave them;
and, sirrah,° I have cases of buckram for the nonce,° to   165
immask our noted outward garments.

PRINCE.   Yea, but I doubt° they will be too hard for us.

POINS.   Well, for two of them, I know them to be as true-bred
cowards as ever turned back; and for the third, if he fight
longer than he sees reason, I'll forswear arms. The virtue   170
of this jest will be the incomprehensible° lies that this

140-42 God . . . move (mimicry again of
the Puritans, who claimed to act only when
the spirit moved them)
144 want countenance   lack   protection
(royal and aristocratic)
146 the (sometimes used in the sixteenth
century for "thou" and "you")
146-47 All-hallow summer (Poins com-
pares Falstaff's youthfulness in old age to
the belated summer that occurs around All
Hallows Day)

151 waylaid   ambushed
157 adventure upon   undertake
161 habits   clothes
161 appointment   piece of equipment
165 sirrah   (term of address showing great
familiarity)
165 cases . . . nonce   outer coverings of
coarse linen for the purpose
167 doubt   fear
171 incomprehensible   unlimited

same fat rogue will tell us when we meet at supper: how
thirty, at least, he fought with; what wards,° what blows,
what extremities he endured; and in the reproof° of this
lives the jest.   175

PRINCE.   Well, I'll go with thee. Provide us all things necessary
and meet me tomorrow night° in Eastcheap. There I'll sup.
Farewell.

POINS.   Farewell, my lord.   *Exit.*

PRINCE..   I know you all, and will awhile uphold°   180
The unyoked humor° of your idleness.
Yet herein will I imitate the sun,°
Who doth permit the base contagious° clouds
To smother up his beauty from the world,
That,° when he please again to be himself,   185
Being wanted,° he may be more wond'red at
By breaking through the foul and ugly mists
Of vapors that did seem to strangle him.
If all the year were playing holidays,
To sport would be as tedious as to work;   190
But when they seldom come, they wished-for come,
And nothing pleaseth but rare accidents.°
So when this loose behavior I throw off
And pay the debt I never promisèd,
By how much better than my word I am,   195
By so much shall I falsify men's hopes;°
And, like bright metal on a sullen ground,°
My reformation, glitt'ring o'er my fault,
Shall show more goodly and attract more eyes
Than that which hath no foil° to set it off.   200
I'll so offend to° make offense a skill,
Redeeming time° when men think least I will.   *Exit.*

---

173 **wards** parries (in swordplay)
174 **reproof** disproof
177 **tomorrow night** (they will meet for
the robbery tomorrow morning, but Hal is
thinking ahead of the jest on Falstaff that
night)
180 **uphold** play along with
181 **unyoked humor** uncontrolled behavior
182 **sun** (royalty's traditional symbol)
183 **contagious** (clouds were thought to
breed pestilence)
185 **That** so that
186 **wanted** lacked, missed
192 **rare accidents** unexpected or uncommon events

196 **hopes** expectations
197 **sullen ground** dull background
200 **foil** contrasting background
201 **to** as to
202 **Redeeming time** making amends (Hal
alludes to Ephesians 5:7 ff, which bears in a
general way on much that has been said in
this scene: "Be not ye therefore partakers
with them, for ye were sometimes darkness,
but now are ye light in the Lord: walk as
children of light . . . See then that ye walk
circumspectly, not as fools, but as wise,
redeeming the time, because the days are
evil")

Enter the King, Northumberland, Worcester,   I iii
Hotspur, Sir Walter Blunt, with others.

KING.   My blood hath been too cold and temperate,
Unapt° to stir at these indignities,
And you have found me,° for accordingly
You tread upon my patience; but be sure
I will from henceforth rather be myself,°   5
Mighty and to be feared, than my condition,°
Which hath been smooth as oil, soft as young down,
And therefore lost that title of respect
Which the proud soul ne'er pays but to the proud.

WORCESTER.   Our house, my sovereign liege, little deserves   10
The scourge of greatness to be used on it—
And that same greatness too which our own hands
Have holp° to make so portly.°

NORTHUMBERLAND.   My lord—

KING.   Worcester, get thee gone, for I do see   15
Danger° and disobedience in thine eye.
O, sir, your presence is too bold and peremptory,
And majesty might never yet endure
The moody frontier° of a servant brow.
You have good leave to leave us: when we need   20
Your use and counsel, we shall send for you.
                                            Exit Worcester.
You were about to speak.

NORTHUMBERLAND.   Yea, my good lord.
Those prisoners in your Highness' name demanded
Which Harry Percy here at Holmedon took,   25
Were, as he says, not with such strength denied
As is deliverèd° to your Majesty.
Either envy,° therefore, or misprision°
Is guilty of this fault, and not my son.

I iii 2 Unapt slow	**16 Danger** defiance
3 found me found me out	**19 frontier** rampart (as if Worcester were
5 myself i.e. what I am as king	an enemy fortress)
6 my condition i.e. what I am by nature	**27 deliverèd** reported
13 holp helped	**28 envy** spite
13 portly stately	**28 misprision** misunderstanding

HOTSPUR.   My liege, I did deny no prisoners.   30
   But I remember, when the fight was done,
   When I was dry with rage and extreme toil,
   Breathless and faint, leaning upon my sword,
   Came there a certain lord, neat and trimly dressed,
   Fresh as a bridegroom, and his chin new reaped°   35
   Showed like a stubble land at harvest home.
   He was perfumèd like a milliner,
   And 'twixt his finger and his thumb he held
   A pouncet° box, which ever and anon°
   He gave° his nose, and took't away again;   40
   Who° therewith angry, when it next came there,
   Took it in snuff;° and still° he smiled and talked;
   And as the soldiers bore dead bodies by,
   He called them untaught knaves, unmannerly,
   To bring a slovenly° unhandsome corpse   45
   Betwixt the wind and his nobility.
   With many holiday and lady° terms
   He questioned° me, amongst the rest° demanded
   My prisoners in your Majesty's behalf.
   I then, all smarting with my wounds being cold,   50
   To be so pest'red with a popingay,°
   Out of my grief° and my impatience
   Answered neglectingly, I know not what—
   He should, or he should not; for he made me mad
   To see him shine so brisk,° and smell so sweet,   55
   And talk so like a waiting gentlewoman
   Of guns and drums and wounds—God save the mark!°—
   And telling me the sovereignest° thing on earth
   Was parmacity° for an inward bruise,
   And that it was great pity, so it was,   60

---

35 reaped i.e. with the closely clipped beard of a man of fashion
39 pouncet perfume
39 ever and anon repeatedly
40 gave held to
41 Who i.e. his nose
42 Took . . . snuff (proverbial, meaning "took offense," but here with pun on "snuffing" the perfume)
42 still continually
45 slovenly befouled
47 holiday and lady fastidious and effeminate

48 questioned talked to
48 rest i.e. the rest of what he said
51 popingay parrot (here, one who is gaudy in dress and chatters emptily)
52 grief pain
55 brisk spruce ("sharp")
57 God . . . mark (a ritual phrase originally used to invoke a blessing, but here expressing scorn)
58 sovereignest most effective
59 parmacity spermaceti (medicinal substance found in sperm whales)

This villainous saltpeter° should be digged
Out of the bowels of the harmless earth,
Which many a good tall° fellow had destroyed
So cowardly, and but for these vile guns
He would himself have been a soldier.   65
This bald unjointed° chat of his, my lord,
I answered indirectly,° as I said,
And I beseech you, let not his report
Come current° for an accusation
Betwixt my love and your high Majesty.   70

BLUNT.   The circumstance consider'd, good my lord,
Whate'er Lord Harry Percy then had said
To such a person, and in such a place,
At such a time, with all the rest retold,
May reasonably die, and never rise   75
To do him wrong,° or any way impeach°
What then he said, so° he unsay it now.

KING.   Why, yet he doth deny his prisoners,
But with proviso and exception,
That we at our own charge shall ransom straight°   80
His brother-in-law, the foolish Mortimer;
Who, on my soul, hath willfully betrayed
The lives of those that he did lead to fight
Against that great magician, damned Glendower—
Whose daughter, as we hear, that Earl of March   85
Hath lately married. Shall our coffers, then,
Be emptied to redeem° a traitor home?
Shall we buy treason, and indent° with fears°
When they have lost and forfeited themselves?
No, on the barren mountains let him starve!   90
For I shall never hold that man my friend
Whose tongue shall ask me for one penny cost
To ransom home revolted° Mortimer.

---

61 **saltpeter** potassium nitrate, basis of
gunpowder
63 **tall** stalwart
66 **bald unjointed** trivial and disjointed
67 **indirectly** offhand
69 **Come current** (1) be accepted (i.e. as
of true coin) (2) intrude
76 **To . . . wrong** i.e. to be held against
him

76 **impeach** call in question
77 **so** so long as
80 **straight** at once
87 **redeem** ransom
88 **indent** bargain
88 **fears** (1) cowards (2) traitors, i.e. those
who by "fear" have yielded to the enemy
and so become traitors "to be feared"
93 **revolted** treasonous

HOTSPUR.   Revolted Mortimer?
He never did fall off, my sovereign liege,   95
But by the chance of war. To prove that true
Needs no more but one tongue for all those wounds,
Those mouthèd wounds,° which valiantly he took
When on the gentle Severn's sedgy bank,
In single opposition hand to hand,   100
He did confound° the best part of an hour
In changing hardiment° with great Glendower.
Three times they breathed,° and three times did they drink,
Upon agreement, of swift Severn's flood;
Who° then affrighted with their bloody looks   105
Ran fearfully among the trembling reeds
And hid his crisp° head in the hollow bank,
Bloodstainèd with these valiant combatants.
Never did bare and rotten policy°
Color° her working with such deadly wounds;   110
Nor never could the noble Mortimer
Receive so many, and all willingly.
Then let not him be slanderèd with revolt.°

KING.   Thou dost belie° him, Percy, thou dost belie him!
He never did encounter with Glendower.   115
I tell thee, he durst as well° have met the devil alone
As Owen Glendower for an enemy.
Art thou not ashamed? But, sirrah,° henceforth
Let me not hear you speak of Mortimer.
Send me your prisoners with the speediest means,   120
Or you shall hear in such a kind from me
As will displease you. My Lord Northumberland,
We license° your departure with your son.
Send us your prisoners, or you will hear of it.
                    Exit King, [with Blunt, and train].

---

98 **mouthèd wounds** i.e. wounds that speak
for him (based on the likeness of a bloody
flesh wound to a mouth)
101 **confound** spend
102 **changing hardiment** exchanging blows
103 **breathed** paused for breath
105 **Who** i.e. the river
107 **crisp** (used punningly to mean both
"curled" [of a man's head] and "rippling"
[of a river]; "head" also refers punningly to
a river's source)

109 **policy** cunning
110 **Color** (1) disguise (2) redden (i.e.
with blood)
113 **revolt** treason
114 **belie** lie about
116 **durst as well** would as soon have
dared
118 **sirrah** (term of address to an inferior,
here insulting)
123 **license** allow

HOTSPUR.   And if° the devil come and roar for them,   125
    I will not send them. I will after° straight
    And tell him so, for I will ease my heart,
    Albeit I make a hazard of° my head.

NORTHUMBERLAND.   What, drunk with choler?° Stay, and
    pause awhile.
    Here comes your uncle.   130

Enter Worcester.

HOTSPUR.   Speak of Mortimer?
    Zounds, I will speak of him, and let my soul
    Want mercy if I do not join with him!
    Yea, on his part I'll empty all these veins,
    And shed my dear blood drop by drop in the dust,   135
    But I will lift the downtrod Mortimer
    As high in the air as this unthankful king,
    As this ingrate and cank'red° Bolingbroke.°

NORTHUMBERLAND.   Brother, the King hath made your nephew
    mad.°

WORCESTER.   Who struck this heat up after I was gone?   140

HOTSPUR.   He will forsooth° have all my prisoners;
    And when I urged the ransom once again
    Of my wife's brother, then his cheek looked pale,
    And on my face he turned an eye of death,°
    Trembling even at the name of Mortimer.   145

WORCESTER.   I cannot blame him. Was not he proclaimed
    By Richard that dead is, the next of blood?°

NORTHUMBERLAND.   He was, I heard the proclamation:
    And then it was when the unhappy king
    (Whose wrongs in us° God pardon!) did set forth   150
    Upon his Irish expedition;
    From whence he intercepted° did return
    To be deposed, and shortly murderèd.

---

125   **And if** even if
126   **after** go after
128   **make . . . of** risk
129   **choler** anger
138   **cank'red** infected (see note 178)
138   **Bolingbroke** i.e. the King
139   **mad** insane (with fury)

141   **forsooth** lit. "in truth" (but here
    more like "Imagine it! What a nerve!")
144   **of death** showing deadly fear
147   **next of blood** i.e. heir to the throne
150   **in us** at our hands
152   **intercepted** interrupted

WORCESTER. And for whose death we in the world's wide
    mouth
    Live scandalized and foully spoken of.   155

HOTSPUR. But soft, I pray you, did King Richard then
    Proclaim my brother° Edmund Mortimer
    Heir to the crown?

NORTHUMBERLAND. He did, myself did hear it.

HOTSPUR. Nay, then I cannot blame his cousin king,   160
    That wished him on the barren mountains starve.
    But shall it be that you, that set the crown
    Upon the head of this forgetful man,
    And for his sake wear the detested blot
    Of murderous subornation°—shall it be   165
    That you a world of curses undergo,
    Being the agents or base second means,
    The cords, the ladder, or the hangman rather?
    O, pardon me that I descend so low
    To show the line° and the predicament°   170
    Wherein you range under this subtle king!
    Shall it for shame be spoken in these days,
    Or fill up chronicles in time to come,
    That men of your nobility and power
    Did gage° them both in an unjust behalf   175
    (As both of you, God pardon it, have done)
    To put down Richard, that sweet lovely rose,
    And plant this thorn, this canker° Bolingbroke?
    And shall it in more shame be further spoken
    That you are fooled,° discarded, and shook off   180
    By him for whom these shames ye underwent?
    No, yet time serves° wherein you may redeem
    Your banished honors and restore yourselves
    Into the good thoughts of the world again;
    Revenge the jeering and disdained contempt   185

---

157 brother i.e. brother-in-law
165 murderous subornation complicity in murder
170 line degree, station (but also "hangman's rope" [see line 168] and "tether" [see line 171])
170 predicament category (but also "perilous position")
175 gage pledge
178 canker dog-rose (an inferior rose, but with suggestions of "cankerworm" and "ulcer")
180 fooled duped
182 yet . . . serves there still is time

Of this proud king, who studies day and night
To answer all the debt he owes to you
Even with the bloody payment of your deaths.°
Therefore I say—

WORCESTER.   Peace, cousin, say no more;   190
And now I will unclasp a secret book,
And to your quick-conceiving° discontents
I'll read you matter deep and dangerous,
As full of peril and adventurous spirit
As to o'erwalk a current roaring loud   195
On the unsteadfast footing of a spear.

HOTSPUR.   If he fall in, good night, or sink, or swim!°
Send danger from the east unto the west,
So° honor cross it from the north to south,
And let them grapple. O, the blood more stirs   200
To rouse a lion than to start a hare!

NORTHUMBERLAND.   Imagination of some great exploit
Drives him beyond the bounds of patience.°

HOTSPUR.   By heaven, methinks it were an easy leap
To pluck bright honor from the pale-faced moon,   205
Or dive into the bottom of the deep,
Where fathom line could never touch the ground,
And pluck up drownèd honor by the locks,
So he that doth redeem her thence might wear
Without corrival° all her dignities;   210
But out upon this half-faced fellowship!°

WORCESTER.   He apprehends° a world of figures° here,
But not the form of what he should attend.
Good cousin, give me audience for a while.

HOTSPUR.   I cry you mercy.°   215

WORCESTER.   Those same noble Scots that are your prisoners—

HOTSPUR.   I'll keep them all.
By God, he shall not have a Scot of them!

---

188 **deaths** (see note V i 127)
192 **quick-conceiving** eagerly responsive
197 **good . . . swim** i.e. the man is doomed whether he sinks at once or is swept away by the current
199 **So** provided
203 **patience** self-restraint
210 **corrival** sharer

211 **out . . . fellowship** down with this half-and-half sharing (of honors)
212 **apprehends** grasps
212 **figures** (1) figures of speech (2) airy fancies (as opposed to substantial "form," line 213)
215 **cry you mercy** beg your pardon

No, if a Scot° would save his soul, he shall not.
I'll keep them, by this hand!   220

WORCESTER.   You start away°
And lend no ear unto my purposes.
Those prisoners you shall keep.

HOTSPUR.   Nay, I will. That's flat!°
He said he would not ransom Mortimer,   225
Forbade my tongue to speak of Mortimer,
But I will find him when he lies asleep,
And in his ear I'll hollo "Mortimer."
Nay, I'll have a starling° shall be taught to speak
Nothing but "Mortimer," and give it him   230
To keep his anger still° in motion.

WORCESTER.   Hear you, cousin, a word.

HOTSPUR.   All studies° here I solemnly defy°
Save how to gall and pinch this Bolingbroke;
And that same sword-and-buckler° Prince of Wales,   235
But that I think his father loves him not
And would be glad he met with some mischance,
I would have him poisonèd with a pot of ale.°

WORCESTER.   Farewell, kinsman: I'll talk to you
When you are better tempered to attend.   240

NORTHUMBERLAND.   Why, what a wasp-stung and impatient
    fool
Art thou to break into this woman's mood,
Tying thine ear to no tongue but thine own!

HOTSPUR.   Why, look you, I am whipped and scourged with
    rods,
Nettled, and stung with pismires,° when I hear   245
Of this vile politician,° Bolingbroke.
In Richard's time—what do you call the place?
A plague upon it! It is in Gloucestershire;
'Twas where the madcap duke his uncle kept,°

---

219 **Scot** (pun on "scot," meaning "small payment")
221 **start away** change the subject
224 **flat** final
229 **starling** a mimicking, crow-like bird
231 **still** constantly
233 **studies** interests
233 **defy** reject

235 **sword-and-buckler** "lowdown" (sword and shield were arms of the lower class)
238 **ale** (a further glance at Hal's presumed low tastes, a gentleman's drink being wine)
245 **pismires** ants
246 **politician** schemer
249 **kept** lived

His uncle York—where I first bowed my knee   250
Unto this king of smiles, this Bolingbroke—
'Sblood!—when you and he came back from
    Ravenspurgh°—

NORTHUMBERLAND.   At Berkeley Castle.

HOTSPUR.   You say true.
Why, what a candy deal° of courtesy   255
This fawning greyhound then did proffer me!
"Look when his infant fortune came to age,"
And "gentle Harry Percy," and "kind cousin"—
O, the devil take such cozeners!°—God forgive me!
Good uncle, tell your tale; I have done.   260

WORCESTER.   Nay, if you have not, to it again.
We will stay your leisure.°

HOTSPUR.   I have done, i' faith.

WORCESTER.   Then once more to your Scottish prisoners:
Deliver them up without their ransom straight,   265
And make the Douglas' son your only mean°
For powers in Scotland—which, for divers reasons
Which I shall send you written, be assured
Will easily be granted. [*to Northumberland*] You, my lord,
Your son in Scotland being thus employed,   270
Shall secretly into the bosom creep
Of that same noble prelate well-beloved,
The Archbishop.

HOTSPUR.   Of York, is it not?

WORCESTER.   True; who bears hard°   275
His brother's death at Bristow,° the Lord Scroop.
I speak not this in estimation,°
As what I think might be, but what I know
Is ruminated, plotted, and set down,
And only stays but to behold the face   280
Of that occasion that shall bring it on.

---

252 Ravenspurgh harbor in Yorkshire (where
Hotspur's father had gone to take sides
with Bolingbroke—who was returning from
exile on the Continent—against the absent
King Richard III)
255 candy deal sugared bit
259 cozeners cheats (with pun on "cousin"
of previous line)

262 stay . . . leisure wait you out
266 mean means
275 bears hard resents (because his brother had been executed by Henry)
276 Bristow Bristol
277 in estimation as a guess

HOTSPUR.   I smell it.° Upon my life, it will do well.

NORTHUMBERLAND.   Before the game is afoot thou still° let'st
  slip.°

HOTSPUR.   Why, it cannot choose° but be a noble plot.
  And then the power of Scotland and of York   285
  To join with Mortimer, ha?

WORCESTER.   And so they shall.

HOTSPUR.   In faith, it is exceedingly well aimed.

WORCESTER.   And 'tis no little reason bids us speed
  To save our heads by raising of a head;°   290
  For, bear ourselves as even° as we can,
  The King will always think him in our debt,
  And think we think ourselves unsatisfied,
  Till he hath found a time to pay us home.°
  And see already how he doth begin   295
  To make us strangers to his looks of love.

HOTSPUR.   He does, he does! We'll be revenged on him.

WORCESTER.   Cousin, farewell. No further go in this
  Than I by letters shall direct your course.
  When time is ripe, which will be suddenly,°   300
  I'll steal to Glendower and Lord Mortimer,
  Where you and Douglas, and our pow'rs at once,
  As I will fashion it, shall happily meet,
  To bear our fortunes in our own strong arms,
  Which now we hold at much uncertainty.   305

NORTHUMBERLAND.   Farewell, good brother. We shall thrive, I
  trust.

HOTSPUR.   Uncle, adieu. O, let the hours be short
  Till fields° and blows and groans applaud our sport!

Exeunt.

❦⁓⁓⁓

---

282 smell it i.e. like a hound catching
the scent
283 still always
283 let'st slip let loose (the dogs)
284 choose help

290 head army
291 even carefully
294 home fully, i.e. with a "home" thrust
300 suddenly speedily
308 fields battlefields

Enter a Carrier° with a lantern in his hand.   II i

FIRST CARRIER.   Heigh-ho! An it be not four by the day,° I'll be
    hanged. Charles' wain° is over the new chimney, and yet
    our horse° not packed. What, ostler!°

OSTLER.   [*within*] Anon,° anon.

FIRST CARRIER.   I prithee, Tom, beat° Cut's saddle, put a few 5
    flocks in the point;° poor jade is wrung in the withers° out
    of all cess.°
                    Enter another Carrier.

SECOND CARRIER.   Peas and beans° are as dank here as a dog,°
    and that is the next° way to give poor jades the bots.° This
    house is turned upside down since Robin Ostler died.   10

FIRST CARRIER.   Poor fellow never joyed since the price of oats
    rose; it was the death of him.

SECOND CARRIER.   I think this be the most villainous house in
    all London road for fleas, I am stung like a tench.°

FIRST CARRIER.   Like a tench? By the mass, there is ne'er a king 15
    christen could be better bit than I have been° since the first
    cock.°

SECOND CARRIER.   Why, they will allow us ne'er a jordan,° and
    then we leak in your chimney,° and your chamber-lye°
    breeds fleas like a loach.°   20

FIRST CARRIER.   What, ostler! Come away° and be hanged!
    Come away!

SECOND CARRIER.   I have a gammon° of bacon and two razes°
    of ginger, to be delivered as far as Charing Cross.°

II i s.d. Carrier person in charge of trans-	**9 bots** worms
porting goods	**14 tench** fish with red spots (as if flea-
1 by the day in the morning	bitten)
2 Charles' wain the Great Bear or Big	**15-16 there . . . been** i.e. not even a
Dipper	Christian king (though kings get the best of
3 horse horses	everything) could have surpassed my record
3 ostler stableman	in flea bites
4 Anon (I'm coming) at once	**16-17 the . . . cock** midnight
5 beat (to soften it)	**18 jordan** chamberpot
5-6 a . . . point a little padding in the	**19 chimney** fireplace
pommel	**19 chamber-lye** urine
6 wrung . . . withers rubbed raw at the	**20 loach** fish that breeds often
shoulders	**21 Come away** come here
6-7 out . . . cess to excess	**23 gammon** haunch
8 Peas and beans horse fodder	**23 razes** roots
8 dank . . . dog i.e. musty as a wet dog	**24 Charing Cross** a London marketplace
9 next surest	

FIRST CARRIER. God's body! The turkeys in my pannier° are 25
quite starved. What, ostler! A plague on thee, hast thou
never an eye in thy head? Canst not hear? And 'twere not
as good deed as drink to break the pate on thee,° I am a
very villain. Come, and be hanged! Hast no faith° in thee?

Enter Gadshill.

GADSHILL. Good morrow, carriers, what's o'clock? 30

FIRST CARRIER. I think it be two o'clock.

GADSHILL. I prithee lend me thy lantern to see my gelding in
the stable.

FIRST CARRIER. Nay, by God, soft!° I know a trick worth two
of that, i' faith. 35

GADSHILL. I pray thee lend me thine.

SECOND CARRIER. Ay, when? Canst tell?° Lend me thy lantern,
quoth he? Marry, I'll see thee hanged first!

GADSHILL. Sirrah carrier, what time do you mean to come to
London? 40

SECOND CARRIER. Time enough to go to bed with a candle,° I
warrant thee. Come, neighbor Mugs, we'll call up the gentlemen, they will along° with company, for they have great
charge.° *Exeunt [Carriers].*

GADSHILL. What, ho! Chamberlain!° 45

Enter Chamberlain.

CHAMBERLAIN. "At hand,° quoth pickpurse."

GADSHILL. That's even as fair as "at hand, quoth the chamberlain"; for thou variest no more from picking of purses than
giving direction doth from laboring: thou layest the plot
how. 50

CHAMBERLAIN. Good morrow, Master Gadshill. It holds cur-
rent° that I told you yesternight: there's a franklin° in the

---

25 **pannier** basket
28 **break . . . thee** break your head
29 **faith** trustworthiness
34 **soft** i.e. "listen to him!"
37 **Ay . . . tell** (standard retort to an in-
opportune request)
41 **Time . . . candle** (evasively spoken,
the carriers being suspicious of Gadshill)
43 **will along** want to go along

44 **charge** luggage
45 **Chamberlain** male servant, like cham-
bermaid
46 **At hand** (a popular tag meaning "Ready,
sir!" but relevant here to the Chamberlain's
filching way of life, as Gadshill points out)
51-52 **current** true
52 **franklin** rich farmer

Wild° of Kent hath brought three hundred marks° with
him in gold, I heard him tell it to one of his company last
night at supper—a kind of auditor,° one that hath abun- 55
dance of charge too, God knows what. They are up already
and call for eggs and butter, they will away presently.

GADSHILL.   Sirrah, if they meet not with Saint Nicholas'
clerks,° I'll give thee this neck.

CHAMBERLAIN.   No, I'll none of it; I pray thee keep that for the 60
hangman; for I know thou worshippest Saint Nicholas as
truly as a man of falsehood may.

GADSHILL.   What talkest thou to me of the hangman? If I
hang, I'll make a fat pair of gallows; for if I hang, old Sir
John hangs with me, and thou knowest he is no starveling. 65
Tut! There are other Troyans° that thou dream'st not of,
the which for sport sake are content to do the profession
some grace; that would (if matters should be looked into)
for their own credit sake make all whole. I am joined
with no foot-landrakers,° no long-staff sixpenny strikers,° 70
none of these mad mustachio purple-hued maltworms;°
but with nobility and tranquillity,° burgomasters and great
oneyers,° such as can hold in,° such as will strike sooner
than speak,° and speak sooner than drink, and drink sooner
than pray—and yet, zounds, I lie, for they pray continually 75
to their saint, the commonwealth,° or rather, not pray to
her, but prey on her, for they ride up and down on her
and make her their boots.°

CHAMBERLAIN.   What, the commonwealth their boots? Will she
hold out water in foul way?°   80

---

53 **Wild** lit. "weald," i.e. uncultivated
upland
53 **three hundred marks** £200 (Elizabethan
value)
55 **auditor** revenue officer
58-59 **Saint . . . clerks** highwaymen (St.
Nicholas was reckoned the patron of all
travelers, including traveling thieves)
66 **Troyans** good fellows
70 **foot-landrakers** footloose vagabonds
70 **long-staff . . . strikers** men who would
pull you from your horse with long staves
even to steal sixpence

71 **mustachio . . . maltworms** big-mus-
tached purple-faced drunkards
72 **tranquillity** (Gadshill's witty coinage,
on the analogy of "nobility": people who
don't have to scrounge their living)
73 **oneyers** ones (?)
73 **hold in** keep their mouths shut
74 **speak** i.e. say "hands up"
76 **commonwealth** the state, society
78 **boots** (with pun on "booty")
80 **in . . . way** on muddy roads

GADSHILL.   She will, she will! Justice hath liquored° her. We steal as in a castle,° cocksure. We have the receipt of fernseed,° we walk invisible.

CHAMBERLAIN.   Nay, by my faith, I think you are more behold-ing to the night than to fernseed for your walking invisible.   85

GADSHILL.   Give me thy hand. Thou shalt have a share in our purchase,° as I am a true man.

CHAMBERLAIN.   Nay, rather let me have it, as you are a false thief.

GADSHILL.   Go to; "homo" is a common name to all men.° Bid   90 the ostler bring my gelding out of the stable. Farewell, you muddy° knave.   [*Exeunt.*]

~⚬~⚬~✗~⚬~⚬~

Enter Prince, Poins, and Peto, etc.   II ii

POINS.   Come, shelter, shelter! I have removed Falstaff's horse, and he frets° like a gummed velvet.

PRINCE.   Stand close.   [*They step aside.*]
Enter Falstaff.

FALSTAFF.   Poins! Poins, and be hanged! Poins!

PRINCE.   [*comes forward*] Peace, ye fat-kidneyed rascal! What   5 a brawling dost thou keep!

FALSTAFF.   Where's Poins, Hal?

PRINCE.   He is walked up to the top of the hill; I'll go seek him.
[*Steps aside.*]

FALSTAFF.   I am accursed to rob in that thief's company. The rascal hath removed my horse and tied him I know not   10 where. If I travel but four foot by the squire° further afoot,

---

81 **liquored** (1) greased (as with boots) (2) made her drunk
82 **as . . . castle** securely
82-83 **receipt of fernseed** recipe of fern-seed (popularly supposed to render one invisible)
87 **purchase** (euphemism for loot)

90 **"homo" . . . men** i.e. "homo" (Latin for man) is a term that applies to all men, true (honest) or false
92 **muddy** rascally
II ii 2 **frets** chafes (with pun on the fret-ting or fraying of velvet as the gum used to stiffen it wore away)
11 **squire** rule

I shall break my wind.° Well, I doubt not but to die a fair
death for all this, if I scape hanging for killing that rogue.
I have forsworn his company hourly any time this two and
twenty years, and yet I am bewitched with the rogue's com-   15
pany. If the rascal have not given me medicines° to make
me love him, I'll be hanged. It could not be else: I have
drunk medicines. Poins! Hal! A plague upon you both!
Bardolph! Peto! I'll starve° ere I'll rob a foot further. And
'twere not as good a deed as drink to turn true° man and   20
to leave these rogues, I am the veriest varlet° that ever
chewed with a tooth. Eight yards of uneven ground is
threescore and ten miles a foot with me, and the stony-
hearted villains know it well enough. A plague upon it
when thieves cannot be true one to another! (*They*   25
whistle.) Whew! A plague upon you all! Give me my horse,
you rogues! Give me my horse and be hanged!

PRINCE.   [*comes forward*] Peace, ye fat-guts! Lie down, lay
thine ear close to the ground, and list if thou canst hear
the tread of travelers.   30

FALSTAFF.   Have you any levers to lift me up again, being
down? 'Sblood, I'll not bear mine own flesh so far afoot
again for all the coin in thy father's exchequer. What a
plague mean ye to colt° me thus?

PRINCE.   Thou liest, thou art not colted, thou art uncolted.°   35

FALSTAFF.   I prithee, good Prince Hal, help me to my horse,
good king's son.

PRINCE.   Out, ye rogue! Shall I be your ostler?

FALSTAFF.   Hang thyself in thine own heir-apparent garters!°
If I be ta'en, I'll peach° for this. And I have not ballads   40
made on you all, and sung to filthy tunes, let a cup of sack
be my poison. When a jest is so forward°—and afoot too—
I hate it.
        Enter Gadshill [and Bardolph].

GADSHILL.   Stand!

---

12 **break my wind** (1) be winded (2)
break wind
16 **medicines** love potions
19 **starve** die
20 **true** honest
21 **varlet** rogue

34 **colt** trick
35 **uncolted** i.e. unhorsed
39 **Hang . . . garters** (Falstaff adapts a
proverbial phrase to fit a crown prince)
40 **peach** inform on you
42 **forward** bold

FALSTAFF.   So I do, against my will.   45

POINS.   O, 'tis our setter;° I know his voice. [*comes forward*]
Bardolph, what news?

BARDOLPH.   Case ye,° case ye! On with your vizards! There's
money of the King's coming down the hill; 'tis going to the
King's exchequer.   50

FALSTAFF.   You lie, ye rogue! 'Tis going to the King's tavern.

GADSHILL.   There's enough to make us all—

FALSTAFF.   To be hanged.

PRINCE.   Sirs, you four shall front them in the narrow lane;
Ned Poins and I will walk lower: if they escape from your   55
encounter, then they light on us.

PETO.   How many be there of them?

GADSHILL.   Some eight or ten.

FALSTAFF.   Zounds, will they not rob us?

PRINCE.   What, a coward, Sir John Paunch?   60

FALSTAFF.   Indeed, I am not John of Gaunt° your grandfather,
but yet no coward, Hal.

PRINCE.   Well, we leave that to the proof.°

POINS.   Sirrah Jack, thy horse stands behind the hedge. When
thou need'st him, there thou shalt find him. Farewell and   65
stand fast.

FALSTAFF.   Now cannot I strike him, if I should be hanged.

PRINCE.   [*aside to Poins*] Ned, where are our disguises?

POINS.   [*aside to Prince*] Here, hard by. Stand close.
                                                      [*Exeunt Prince and Poins.*]

FALSTAFF.   Now, my masters, happy man be his dole,° say I.   70
Every man to his business.

Enter the Travelers.

TRAVELER.   Come, neighbor. The boy shall lead our horses
down the hill; we'll walk afoot awhile and ease our legs.

---

46 setter one who arranges a robbery
48 Case ye i.e. encase ye, mask yourselves
61 John of Gaunt Hal's grandfather (but
in reply to "Sir John Paunch" Falstaff puns
on "gaunt" [thin] which Hal evidently is
[see II iv 228-31])

63 proof test
70 happy . . . dole may happiness be our
lot

THIEVES.   Stand!

TRAVELER.   Jesus bless us!   75

FALSTAFF.   Strike! Down with them! Cut the villains' throats!
Ah, whoreson caterpillars!° Bacon-fed knaves! They hate us
youth. Down with them! Fleece them!

TRAVELER.   O, we are undone, both we and ours forever!

FALSTAFF.   Hang ye, gorbellied° knaves, are ye undone? No, ye   80
fat chuffs;° I would your store° were here! On, bacons, on!
What, ye knaves, young men must live. You are grandjurors,° are ye? We'll jure ye, faith!

> *Here they rob them and bind them. Exeunt.*
>
> *Enter the Prince and Poins [disguised].*

PRINCE.   The thieves have bound the true men. Now could thou
and I rob the thieves and go merrily to London, it would   85
be argument° for a week, laughter for a month, and a good
jest forever.

POINS.   Stand close! I hear them coming.   [*They stand aside.*]

> *Enter the thieves again.*

FALSTAFF.   Come, my masters, let us share, and then to horse
before day. And the Prince and Poins be not two arrant°   90
cowards, there's no equity stirring.° There's no more valor
in that Poins than in a wild duck.

PRINCE.   Your money!

POINS.   Villains!

> *As they are sharing, the Prince and
> Poins set upon them. They all run
> away, and Falstaff, after a blow or
> two, runs away too, leaving the
> booty behind them.*

PRINCE.   Got with much ease. Now merrily to horse. The   95
thieves are all scattered, and possessed with fear so strongly
that they dare not meet each other: each takes his fellow

---

77 **whoreson caterpillars** miserable parasites
80 **gorbellied** great-bellied
81 **chuffs** misers
81 **your store** all you own
82-83 **grandjurors** i.e. men of substance
(as required for service on a grand jury)
86 **be argument** make conversation
90 **arrant** thorough
91 **no . . . stirring** i.e. no justice left alive

for an officer. Away, good Ned. Falstaff sweats to death
and lards the lean earth as he walks along. Were't not for
laughing, I should pity him.°   100

POINS.   How the fat rogue roared!   *Exeunt.*

❦

Enter Hotspur solus,° reading a letter.   II iii

HOTSPUR.   "But, for mine own part, my lord, I could be well
contented to be there, in respect of the love I bear your
house.°" He could be contented—why is he not then? In
respect of the love he bears our house! He shows in this
he loves his own barn better than he loves our house. Let   5
me see some more. "The purpose you undertake is dangerous"—why, that's certain! 'Tis dangerous to take a cold,
to sleep, to drink; but I tell you, my lord fool, out of this
nettle,° danger, we pluck this flower, safety. "The purpose
you undertake is dangerous, the friends you have named   10
uncertain, the time itself unsorted,° and your whole plot
too light for the counterpoise of° so great an opposition."
Say you so, say you so? I say unto you again, you are a
shallow, cowardly hind,° and you lie. What a lack-brain is
this! By the Lord, our plot is a good plot as ever was laid; 15
our friends true and constant: a good plot, good friends,
and full of expectation;° an excellent plot, very good
friends. What a frosty-spirited rogue is this! Why, my Lord
of York° commends the plot and the general course of the
action. Zounds, and I were now by this rascal, I could brain 20
him with this lady's fan. Is there not my father, my uncle,
and myself; Lord Edmund Mortimer, my Lord of York, and
Owen Glendower? Is there not, besides, the Douglas? Have
I not all their letters to meet me in arms by the ninth of

95-100 Got . . . him (printed as verse by
Pope and many later editors, with line
breaks after "horse/fear/other/officer/death/
along/him")
II iii s.d. solus alone
3 house family
9 nettle a prickly plant

11 unsorted badly chosen
12 for . . . of to counterbalance
14 hind menial
17 expectation promise
18-19 my . . . York the Archbishop of
York (see I iii 269 ff)

the next month, and are they not some of them set for- 25
ward already? What a pagan° rascal is this, an infidel! Ha!
you shall see now, in very sincerity of fear and cold heart
will he to the King and lay open all our proceedings. O, I
could divide myself and go to buffets° for moving such a
dish of skim milk with so honorable an action! Hang him, 30
let him tell the King! We are prepared. I will set forward
tonight.

Enter his Lady.

How now, Kate? I must leave you within these two hours.

LADY.   O my good lord, why are you thus alone?
For what offense have I this fortnight been   35
A banished woman from my Harry's bed?
Tell me, sweet lord, what is't that takes from thee
Thy stomach,° pleasure, and thy golden sleep?
Why dost thou bend thine eyes upon the earth,
And start so often when thou sit'st alone?   40
Why hast thou lost the fresh blood in thy cheeks
And given my treasures and my rights of thee
To thick-eyed musing and cursed° melancholy?
In thy faint slumbers I by thee have watched,°
And heard thee murmur tales of iron wars,   45
Speak terms of manage° to thy bounding steed,
Cry "Courage! To the field!" And thou hast talked
Of sallies and retires, of trenches, tents,
Of palisadoes,° frontiers,° parapets,
Of basilisks,° of cannon, culverin,°   50
Of prisoners' ransom, and of soldiers slain,
And all the currents° of a heady° fight.
Thy spirit within thee hath been so at war,
And thus hath so bestirred thee in thy sleep,
That beads of sweat have stood upon thy brow   55
Like bubbles in a late-disturbèd stream,
And in thy face strange motions° have appeared,
Such as we see when men restrain their breath

---

26 **pagan** faithless
29 **divide . . . buffets** split myself into
two, and set the halves fighting
38 **stomach** appetite
43 **cursed** peevish
44 **watched** lain awake
46 **manage** horsemanship
49 **palisadoes** defenses made of stakes

49 **frontiers** fortifications
50 **basilisks, culverin** (sizes and types of
cannon)
52 **currents** occurrences
52 **heady** reckless (headstrong)
57 **motions** (1) emotions (?) (2) movements (?)

On some great sudden hest.° O, what portents are these?
Some heavy° business hath my lord in hand,   60
And I must know it, else he loves me not.

HOTSPUR.   What, ho!

[*Enter a Servant.*]

Is Gilliams with the packet gone?

SERVANT.   He is, my lord, an hour ago.

HOTSPUR.   Hath Butler brought those horses from the sheriff?   65

SERVANT.   One horse, my lord, he brought even now.

HOTSPUR.   What horse? A roan, a crop-ear, is it not?

SERVANT.   It is, my lord.

HOTSPUR.   That roan shall be my throne. Well, I will back him
straight. O Esperance!° Bid Butler lead him forth into the   70
park.°   [*Exit Servant.*]

LADY.   But hear you, my lord.

HOTSPUR.   What say'st thou, my lady?

LADY.   What is it carries you away?°

HOTSPUR.   Why, my horse, my love—my horse!   75

LADY.   Out, you mad-headed ape! A weasel hath not such a
deal of spleen° as you are tossed with. In faith, I'll know
your business, Harry, that I will! I fear my brother Mortimer doth stir about his title° and hath sent for you to line°
his enterprise; but if you go°—   80

HOTSPUR.   So far afoot, I shall be weary, love.

LADY.   Come, come, you paraquito,° answer me directly unto
this question that I ask. In faith, I'll break thy little finger,
Harry, and if thou wilt not tell me all things true.°

HOTSPUR.   Away, away, you trifler! Love? I love thee not;   85
I care not for thee, Kate. This is no world

---

59 hest (1) command (?) (2) resolution (?)
60 heavy dreadful
70 Esperance hope (part of the Percy
motto)
69-71 That . . . park (Pope and many later
editors print as verse, with line breaks after
"throne/Esperance/park")
74 away (1) i.e. from home (2) from
your usual self
77 spleen caprice

79 his title i.e. his claim to Henry's
throne (see I iii 156-68)
79 line strengthen
76-80 Out . . . go (printed by Pope and
many later editors as verse, but with a
variety of lineations)
82 paraquito parrot
82-84 Come . . . true (printed by Pope
and many later editors as verse, with line
breaks after "me/ask/Harry/true")

To play with mammets° and to tilt° with lips.
We must have bloody noses and cracked crowns,°
And pass them current too. Gods me,° my horse!
What say'st thou, Kate? What wouldst thou have with me?   90

LADY.   Do you not love me? Do you not indeed?
Well, do not then; for since you love me not,
I will not love myself. Do you not love me?
Nay, tell me if you speak in jest or no.

HOTSPUR.   Come, wilt thou see me ride?   95
And when I am a-horseback, I will swear
I love thee infinitely. But hark you, Kate:
I must not have you henceforth question me
Whither I go, nor reason whereabout.
Whither I must, I must, and—to conclude,   100
This evening must I leave you, gentle Kate.
I know you wise—but yet no farther wise
Than Harry Percy's wife; constant you are—
But yet a woman; and for secrecy,
No lady closer—for I well believe   105
Thou wilt not utter what thou dost not know,
And so far will I trust thee, gentle Kate—

LADY.   How? So far?

HOTSPUR.   Not an inch further. But hark you, Kate:
Whither I go, thither shall you go too;   110
Today will I set forth, tomorrow you.
Will this content you, Kate?

LADY.   It must of force.°   *Exeunt.*

---

87 **mammets** dolls
87 **tilt** duel
88 **crowns** (1) heads (2) coins—which
when "cracked" were hard to "pass current" (possibly there is an allusion to the
"crown" of kingship, which, though not
genuine when usurped, may be passed current by force)
89 **Gods me** God save me
113 **of force** of necessity

Enter Prince and Poins.°   II iv

PRINCE. Ned, prithee come out of that fat° room and lend me
thy hand to laugh a little.

POINS. Where hast been, Hal?

PRINCE. With three or four loggerheads° amongst three or
fourscore hogsheads. I have sounded the very bass-string 5
of humility. Sirrah, I am sworn brother to a leash° of
drawers° and can call them all by their christen names, as
Tom, Dick, and Francis. They take it already upon their
salvation° that, though I be but Prince of Wales, yet I am
the king of courtesy, and tell me flatly I am no proud Jack° 10
like Falstaff, but a Corinthian,° a lad of mettle, a good boy
(by the Lord, so they call me!), and when I am King of
England I shall command all the good lads in Eastcheap.
They call drinking deep, dyeing scarlet;° and when you
breathe in your watering,° they cry "hem!" and bid you 15
play it off.° To conclude, I am so good a proficient in one
quarter of an hour that I can drink with any tinker in his
own language during my life. I tell thee, Ned, thou hast
lost much honor that thou wert not with me in this action.
But, sweet Ned—to sweeten which name of Ned, I give 20
thee this pennyworth of sugar,° clapped even now into my
hand by an under-skinker,° one that never spake other
English in his life than "Eight shillings and sixpence," and
"You are welcome," with this shrill addition, "Anon, anon,
sir! Score° a pint of bastard° in the Half-moon,"° or so— 25
but, Ned, to drive away the time till Falstaff come, I
prithee do thou stand in some by-room while I question my
puny drawer to what end he gave me the sugar; and do

II iv s.d. Enter . . . Poins (they meet in a
tavern which is said to be in Eastcheap
[I ii 119-20], but is never explicitly named;
references to a boar in *Henry IV, Part Two*
suggest it is the Boar's Head)
1 fat hot
4 loggerheads blockheads
6 leash trio
7 drawers tapsters
8-9 take . . . salvation pledge their salvation
10 Jack fellow
11 Corinthian Elizabethan slang: good
sport; one of the boys (see "good boy" in
same line)

14 dyeing scarlet i.e. from the complex-
ion it gives a man
15 breathe . . . watering pause for breath
while drinking
16 play it off down it
21 sugar i.e. for sweetening wine (see
I ii 104)
22 under-skinker under-tapster
25 Score chalk up
25 bastard Spanish wine
25 Half-moon one of the inn's rooms

thou never leave calling "Francis!" that his tale to me may
be nothing but "Anon!" Step aside, and I'll show thee a   30
precedent.°

POINS.   Francis!

PRINCE.   Thou art perfect.

POINS.   Francis!   [*Poins steps aside.*]
           Enter [Francis, a] Drawer.

FRANCIS.   Anon, anon, sir. Look down into the Pomgarnet,°   35
Ralph.

PRINCE.   Come hither, Francis.

FRANCIS.   My lord?

PRINCE.   How long hast thou to serve,° Francis?

FRANCIS.   Forsooth, five years, and as much as to—   40

POINS.   [*within*] Francis!

FRANCIS.   Anon, anon, sir.

PRINCE.   Five year! By'r Lady,° a long lease for the clinking of
pewter. But, Francis, darest thou be so valiant as to play
the coward with thy indenture° and show it a fair pair of   45
heels and run from it?

FRANCIS.   O Lord, sir, I'll be sworn upon all the books° in
England I could find in my heart—

POINS.   [*within*] Francis!

FRANCIS.   Anon, sir.   50

PRINCE.   How old art thou, Francis?

FRANCIS.   Let me see: about Michaelmas° next I shall be—

POINS.   [*within*] Francis!

FRANCIS.   Anon, sir. Pray stay a little, my lord.

PRINCE.   Nay, but hark you, Francis. For the sugar thou gavest   55
me—'twas a pennyworth, was't not?

FRANCIS.   O Lord! I would it had been two!

PRINCE.   I will give thee for it a thousand pound. Ask me
when thou wilt, and thou shalt have it.

---

31   **precedent** example
35   **Pomgarnet** Pomegranate (another of
the inn's rooms)
39   **serve** i.e. as an apprentice (apprentice-
ship ran for seven years)

43   **By'r Lady** by Our Lady (mild oath)
45   **indenture** contract
47   **books** i.e. Bibles
52   **Michaelmas** September 29

POINS. [*within*] Francis!   60

FRANCIS. Anon, anon.

PRINCE. Anon, Francis?° No, Francis; but tomorrow, Francis; or, Francis, a° Thursday; or indeed, Francis, when thou wilt. But, Francis—

FRANCIS. My lord?   65

PRINCE. Wilt thou rob° this leathern-jerkin, crystal-button, not-pated, agate-ring, puke-stocking, caddis-garter, smooth-tongue, Spanish-pouch?°

FRANCIS. O Lord, sir, who do you mean?

PRINCE. Why then, your brown bastard is your only drink; for 70 look you, Francis, your white canvas doublet will sully. In Barbary, sir, it cannot come to so much.°

FRANCIS. What, sir?

POINS. [*within*] Francis!

PRINCE. Away, you rogue! Dost thou not hear them call?   75

Here they both call him. The Drawer stands
amazed, not knowing which way to go.
Enter Vintner.°

VINTNER. What, stand'st thou still, and hear'st such a calling? Look to the guests within. [*Exit Francis.*] My lord, old Sir John, with half a dozen more, are at the door. Shall I let them in?

PRINCE. Let them alone awhile, and then open the door. [*Exit* 80 *Vintner.*] Poins!

POINS. [*within*] Anon, anon, sir.

Enter Poins.

PRINCE. Sirrah, Falstaff and the rest of the thieves are at the door. Shall we be merry?

---

62 **Anon, Francis?** (Hal pretends to take Francis's "anon"—at once—to Poins as meaning he wants the thousand pounds at once)
63 **a** on
66 **rob** i.e. by running away
66-68 **this . . . Spanish-pouch** i.e. the innkeeper, whose middle-class appearance Hal details: leather jacket with crystal buttons, short hair, agate ring, wool stockings, plain worsted (not fancy) garters, ingratiating (and probably unctuous) speech, money pouch of Spanish leather
70-72 **Why . . . much** (semi-nonsense, but the implication seems clear that Francis must stick to his trade)
75 **s.d. Vintner** the innkeeper

POINS.   As merry as crickets, my lad. But hark ye; what cun- 85
ning match have you made with this jest of the drawer?°
Come, what's the issue?°

PRINCE.   I am now of all humors that have showed themselves
humors since the old days of goodman Adam to the pupil
age of this present twelve o'clock at midnight.°   90

[Enter Francis.]

What's o'clock, Francis?

FRANCIS.   Anon, anon, sir.   *[Exit.]*

PRINCE.   That ever this fellow should have fewer words than a
parrot, and yet the son of a woman! His industry is up-
stairs and downstairs, his eloquence the parcel of a reckon- 95
ing.° I am not yet of Percy's mind, the Hotspur of the
North: he that kills me some six or seven dozen of Scots
at a breakfast, washes his hands, and says to his wife, "Fie
upon this quiet life! I want work." "O my sweet Harry,"
says she, "how many hast thou killed today?" "Give my   100
roan horse a drench,"° says he, and answers "Some fourteen," an hour after, "a trifle, a trifle." I prithee call in
Falstaff. I'll play Percy, and that damned brawn° shall play
Dame Mortimer his wife. "Rivo!"° says the drunkard. Call
in Ribs, call in Tallow.   105

Enter Falstaff, [Gadshill, Bardolph, and
Peto; Francis follows with wine].

POINS.   Welcome, Jack. Where hast thou been?

FALSTAFF.   A plague of° all cowards, I say, and a vengeance
too! Marry and amen! Give me a cup of sack, boy. Ere I
lead this life long, I'll sew netherstocks,° and mend them
and foot them too. A plague of all cowards! Give me a cup 110
of sack, rogue. Is there no virtue extant?   *He drinketh.*

PRINCE.   Didst thou never see Titan° kiss a dish of butter (piti-
ful-hearted Titan!) that melted at the sweet tale of the
sun's? If thou didst, then behold that compound.

85-86 what . . . drawer? what's the point
of this game with the drawer?
87 issue outcome, point (of the jest)
88-90 I . . . midnight I am ready for
every kind of gaiety that men have invented
since the beginning of the world
94-96 His . . . reckoning his whole activity is running up and down stairs, his whole
conversation the totaling of bills

101 drench dose of medicine
103 brawn fat boar
104 Rivo (drinking cry of uncertain meaning)
107 of on
109 netherstocks stockings
112 Titan the sun (of which Hal is possibly reminded by Falstaff's broad face, and
his melting effect on the sack)

FALSTAFF. You rogue, here's lime° in this sack too! There is 115
nothing but roguery to be found in villainous man. Yet a
coward is worse than a cup of sack with lime in it—a
villainous coward! Go thy ways, old Jack, die when thou
wilt; if manhood, good manhood, be not forgot upon the
face of the earth, then am I a shotten herring.° There lives 120
not three good men unhanged in England; and one of them
is fat, and grows old. God help the while! A bad world, I
say. I would I were a weaver; I could sing psalms° or anything. A plague of all cowards, I say still!

PRINCE. How now, woolsack? What mutter you? 125

FALSTAFF. A king's son! If I do not beat thee out of thy kingdom with a dagger of lath° and drive all thy subjects afore
thee like a flock of wild geese, I'll never wear hair on my
face more. You Prince of Wales?

PRINCE. Why, you whoreson round man, what's the matter? 130

FALSTAFF. Are not you a coward? Answer me to that—and
Poins there?

POINS. Zounds, ye fat paunch, and ye call me coward, by the
Lord, I'll stab thee.

FALSTAFF. I call thee coward? I'll see thee damned ere I call 135
thee coward, but I would give a thousand pound I could
run as fast as thou canst. You are straight enough in the
shoulders; you care not who sees your back. Call you that
backing of your friends? A plague upon such backing, give
me them that will face me. Give me a cup of sack. I am a 140
rogue if I drunk° today.

PRINCE. O villain, thy lips are scarce wiped since thou drunk'st
last.

FALSTAFF. All is one for that. (*He drinketh.*) A plague of all
cowards, still say I. 145

PRINCE. What's the matter?

---

115 lime (added to make poor wine seem
dry and clear)
120 shotten herring herring that has cast
its roe (and is therefore long and lean)
122-23 God . . . psalms (Falstaff reassumes
his role of comic Puritan. English weavers
were often psalm-singing Protestants who
had fled the Roman Catholic continent)

127 dagger of lath wooden dagger (by
this phrase Falstaff associates himself with
a character called "the Vice" in the old
religious plays who drove the devil off-
stage by beating him with a wooden dagger)
141 drunk have drunk

FALSTAFF.   What's the matter? There be four of us here have
    ta'en a thousand pound this day morning.

PRINCE.   Where is it, Jack, where is it?

FALSTAFF.   Where is it? Taken from us it is. A hundred upon   150
    poor four of us!

PRINCE.   What, a hundred, man?

FALSTAFF.   I am a rogue if I were not at half-sword° with a
    dozen of them two hours together. I have scaped by mira-
    cle. I am eight times thrust through the doublet,° four   155
    through the hose;° my buckler cut through and through;
    my sword hacked like a handsaw—*ecce signum!*° I never
    dealt° better since I was a man. All would not do. A plague
    of all cowards! Let them speak. If they speak more or less
    than truth, they are villains and the sons of darkness.°   160

PRINCE.   Speak, sirs. How was it?

GADSHILL.   We four set upon some dozen—

FALSTAFF.   Sixteen at least, my lord.

GADSHILL.   And bound them.

PETO.   No, no, they were not bound.   165

FALSTAFF.   You rogue, they were bound, every man of them, or
    I am a Jew else—an Ebrew Jew.

GADSHILL.   As we were sharing, some six or seven fresh men
    set upon us—

FALSTAFF.   And unbound the rest, and then come in the other.°   170

PRINCE.   What, fought you with them all?

FALSTAFF.   All? I know not what you call all, but if I fought not
    with fifty of them, I am a bunch of radish!° If there were
    not two or three and fifty° upon poor old Jack, then am I
    no two-legged creature.   175

PRINCE.   Pray God you have not murd'red some of them.

---

153 **at half-sword** infighting at close quarters
155 **doublet** Elizabethan upper garment
156 **hose** Elizabethan breeches
157 **ecce signum** behold the evidence
(spoken as he shows his sword)
158 **dealt** i.e. dealt blows
160 **sons of darkness** i.e. damned (but see
also I ii 23)

170 **other** others
173 **bunch of radish** (again an object long
and lean)
174 **three and fifty** (fifty-three was the
number of Spanish ships popularly reputed
to have opposed Sir Richard Grenville at
the battle of the Azores in 1591; Falstaff
thus humorously claims for his fight the
status of a national epic)

FALSTAFF.   Nay, that's past praying for. I have peppered° two
of them. Two I am sure I have paid,° two rogues in buckram suits. I tell thee what, Hal—if I tell thee a lie, spit in
my face, call me horse. Thou knowest my old ward:°   180
here I lay,° and thus I bore° my point. Four rogues in
buckram let drive at me.

PRINCE.   What, four? Thou saidst but two even now.

FALSTAFF.   Four, Hal. I told thee four.

POINS.   Ay, ay, he said four.   185

FALSTAFF.   These four came all afront° and mainly° thrust at
me. I made me no more ado but took all their seven points
in my target, thus.

PRINCE.   Seven? Why, there were but four even now.

FALSTAFF.   In buckram?   190

POINS.   Ay, four in buckram suits.

FALSTAFF.   Seven, by these hilts, or I am a villain else.

PRINCE.   [*aside to Poins*] Prithee let him alone. We shall have
more anon.

FALSTAFF.   Dost thou hear me, Hal?   195

PRINCE.   Ay, and mark° thee too, Jack.

FALSTAFF.   Do so, for it is worth the list'ning to. These nine in
buckram that I told thee of—

PRINCE.   So, two more already.

FALSTAFF.   Their points being broken—   200

POINS.   Down fell their hose.°

FALSTAFF.   Began to give me ground; but I followed me close,
came in, foot and hand, and with a thought° seven of the
eleven I paid.

PRINCE.   O monstrous!° Eleven buckram men grown out of two! 205

---

177 **peppered** beaten severely and probably killed
178 **paid** settled with
180 **ward** defensive dueling stance
181 **lay** stood
181 **bore** thrust
186 **afront** abreast
186 **mainly** mightily

196 **mark** pay close attention to
201 **Down . . . hose** (Poins wittily takes
"points" in the sense of laces holding the
breeches to the doublet)
203 **with a thought** quick as a thought
205 **monstrous** i.e. (1) in being gigantic
and (2) in making eleven men grow (like
a monster) out of two

FALSTAFF. But, as the devil would have it, three misbegotten
knaves in Kendal green° came at my back and let drive at
me; for it was so dark, Hal, that thou couldest not see
thy hand.

PRINCE. These lies are like their father that begets them—   210
gross as a mountain, open, palpable. Why, thou clay-
brained guts, thou knotty-pated° fool, thou whoreson
obscene greasy tallow-catch°—

FALSTAFF. What, art thou mad? Art thou mad? Is not the truth
the truth?   215

PRINCE. Why, how couldst thou know these men in Kendal
green when it was so dark thou couldst not see thy hand?
Come, tell us your reason. What sayest thou to this?

POINS. Come, your reason, Jack, your reason.

FALSTAFF. What, upon compulsion? Zounds, and I were at the   220
strappado° or all the racks in the world, I would not tell
you on compulsion. Give you a reason on compulsion? If
reasons° were as plentiful as blackberries, I would give
no man a reason upon compulsion, I.

PRINCE. I'll be no longer guilty of this sin; this sanguine°   225
coward, this bed-presser, this horseback-breaker, this huge
hill of flesh—

FALSTAFF. 'Sblood, you starveling, you eel-skin, you dried
neat's-tongue,° you bull's pizzle,° you stockfish°—O for
breath to utter what is like thee!—you tailor's yard, you   230
sheath, you bowcase, you vile standing tuck!°

PRINCE. Well, breathe awhile, and then to it again; and when
thou hast tired thyself in base comparisons, hear me speak
but this.

POINS. Mark, Jack.   235

PRINCE. We two saw you four set on four, and bound them
and were masters of their wealth. Mark now how a plain

---

207 Kendal green a green woolen (called
Kendal from its place of manufacture in
Westmoreland)
212 knotty-pated blockheaded
213 tallow-catch (1) pan to catch drip-
pings under roasting meat (?) (2) tallow-
keech, i.e. roll of fat for making candles (?)
221 strappado kind of torture instrument

223 reasons (pronounced like "raisins,"
and hence comparable to blackberries)
225 sanguine ruddy (and hence valorous-
seeming)
229 neat's-tongue ox-tongue
229 pizzle penis
229 stockfish dried codfish
231 standing tuck upright rapier

tale shall put you down. Then did we two set on you four
and, with a word,° outfaced° you from your prize, and
have it; yea, and can show it you here in the house. And, 240
Falstaff, you carried your guts away as nimbly, with as
quick dexterity, and roared for mercy, and still run and
roared, as ever I heard bullcalf. What a slave art thou to
hack thy sword as thou hast done, and then say it was in
fight! What trick, what device, what starting hole° canst 245
thou now find out to hide thee from this open and apparent
shame?

POINS.   Come, let's hear, Jack. What trick hast thou now?

FALSTAFF.   By the Lord, I knew ye as well as he that made ye.
Why, hear you, my masters. Was it for me to kill the heir 250
apparent? Should I turn upon the true prince? Why, thou
knowest I am as valiant as Hercules, but beware instinct.
The lion will not touch the true prince.° Instinct is a great
matter. I was now a coward on instinct. I shall think the
better of myself, and thee, during my life—I for a valiant 255
lion, and thou for a true prince. But, by the Lord, lads, I
am glad you have the money. Hostess, clap to° the doors.
Watch tonight, pray tomorrow.° Gallants, lads, boys, hearts
of gold, all the titles of good fellowship come to you! What,
shall we be merry? Shall we have a play extempore?° 260

PRINCE.   Content—and the argument° shall be thy running
away.

FALSTAFF.   Ah, no more of that, Hal, and thou lovest me!

Enter Hostess.

HOSTESS.   O Jesu, my lord the Prince!

PRINCE.   How now, my lady the hostess? What say'st thou to 265
me?

HOSTESS.   Marry, my lord, there is a nobleman of the court at
door would speak with you. He says he comes from your
father.

---

239 **with a word** (1) in brief (?) (2) with
a mere shout to scare you (?)
239 **outfaced** scared away
245 **starting hole** hiding place
253 **The lion . . . prince** (a traditional be-
lief about lions)
257 **clap to** shut

258 **Watch . . . tomorrow** (see Matthew
26:41, "Watch and pray, that ye enter not
into temptation"; Falstaff puns on "watch,"
which means "carouse" as well as "keep
vigil")
260 **have . . . extempore** improvise a
play
261 **argument** subject

PRINCE.   Give him as much as will make him a royal man,° 270
and send him back again to my mother.

FALSTAFF.   What manner of man is he?

HOSTESS.   An old man.

FALSTAFF.   What doth gravity° out of his bed at midnight?
Shall I give him his answer?   275

PRINCE.   Prithee do, Jack.

FALSTAFF.   Faith, and I'll send him packing.   *Exit.*

PRINCE.   Now, sirs. By'r Lady, you fought fair; so did you, Peto;
so did you, Bardolph. You are lions too, you ran away upon
instinct, you will not touch the true prince; no—fie!   280

BARDOLPH.   Faith, I ran when I saw others run.

PRINCE.   Faith, tell me now in earnest, how came Falstaff's
sword so hacked?

PETO.   Why, he hacked it with his dagger, and said he would
swear truth out of England but he would make you believe 285
it was done in fight, and persuaded us to do the like.

BARDOLPH.   Yea, and to tickle our noses with speargrass to
make them bleed, and then to beslubber our garments with
it and swear it was the blood of true men. I did that° I did
not this seven year before—I blushed to hear his monstrous 290
devices.

PRINCE.   O villain! Thou stolest a cup of sack eighteen years
ago and wert taken with the manner,° and ever since thou
hast blushed extempore.° Thou hadst fire and sword on thy
side, and yet thou ran'st away. What instinct hadst thou 295
for it?

BARDOLPH.   My lord, do you see these meteors?° Do you behold
these exhalations?°

PRINCE.   I do.

BARDOLPH.   What think you they portend?   300

---

270 **royal man** (see "noble" in the previous speech, but with a pun on the "royal," a coin worth ten shillings, which was of greater value than the "noble," worth six shillings eight pence)
274 **gravity** i.e. sober age
289 **that** what
293 **taken . . . manner** caught with the goods

294 **extempore** all the time (alluding to the glowing red face or "fire" of the heavy drinker)
297-98 **meteors, exhalations** the pimples and other features of Bardolph's face, spoken of as if they were meteorological portents

PRINCE. Hot livers and cold purses.°

BARDOLPH. Choler,° my lord, if rightly taken.

PRINCE. No, if rightly taken, halter.

Enter Falstaff.

Here comes lean Jack; here comes bare-bone. How now,
my sweet creature of bombast?° How long is't ago, Jack, 305
since thou sawest thine own knee?

FALSTAFF. My own knee? When I was about thy years, Hal, I
was not an eagle's talent° in the waist; I could have crept
into any alderman's thumb-ring. A plague of sighing and
grief, it blows a man up like a bladder. There's villainous 310
news abroad. Here was Sir John Bracy from your father:
you must to the court in the morning. That same mad
fellow of the north, Percy, and he of Wales that gave
Amamon the bastinado, and made Lucifer cuckold, and
swore the devil his true liegeman upon the cross of a Welsh 315
hook°—what a plague call you him?

POINS. Owen Glendower.

FALSTAFF. Owen, Owen—the same; and his son-in-law Mortimer, and old Northumberland, and that sprightly Scot of
Scots, Douglas, that runs a-horseback up a hill perpen- 320
dicular—

PRINCE. He that rides at high speed and with his pistol kills
a sparrow flying.

FALSTAFF. You have hit it.

PRINCE. So did he never the sparrow. 325

FALSTAFF. Well, that rascal hath good metal° in him; he will
not run.

PRINCE. Why, what a rascal art thou then, to praise him so
for running!

---

301 Hot . . . purses (the two notable
results of excessive drink)
302 Choler anger (Bardolph implies that
he is choleric, and therefore no coward;
Hal proceeds to understand "choler" as
"collar," which in Bardolph's case will be
—if "rightly taken"—the hangman's noose)
305 bombast cotton stuffing
308 talent talon

313-16 he of Wales . . . hook (Falstaff alludes to Glendower's supposed magical
powers: he has cudgled a devil named
Amamon, made horns grow on Lucifer, and
forced the devil to swear allegiance to him
on the cross of a weapon that has no
cross)
326 good metal (with pun on "mettle,"
spirit, courage)

FALSTAFF.   A-horseback, ye cuckoo! But afoot he will not budge   330
a foot.

PRINCE.   Yes, Jack, upon instinct.

FALSTAFF.   I grant ye, upon instinct. Well, he is there too, and
one Mordake, and a thousand bluecaps° more. Worcester
is stol'n away tonight; thy father's beard is turned white   335
with the news; you may buy land now as cheap as stinking
mack'rel.

PRINCE.   Why then, it is like, if there come a hot June, and this
civil buffeting hold, we shall buy maidenheads as they buy
hobnails, by the hundreds.°   340

FALSTAFF.   By the mass, lad, thou sayest true; it is like we shall
have good trading that way. But tell me, Hal, art not thou
horrible afeard? Thou being heir apparent, could the world
pick thee out three such enemies again as that fiend
Douglas, that spirit° Percy, and that devil Glendower? Art   345
thou not horribly afraid? Doth not thy blood thrill° at it?

PRINCE.   Not a whit, i' faith. I lack some of thy instinct.

FALSTAFF.   Well, thou wilt be horribly chid tomorrow when
thou comest to thy father. If thou love me, practice an
answer.   350

PRINCE.   Do thou stand for my father and examine me upon
the particulars of my life.

FALSTAFF.   Shall I? Content. This chair shall be my state,°
this dagger my scepter, and this cushion my crown.

PRINCE.   Thy state is taken for° a joined-stool, thy golden   355
scepter for a leaden dagger, and thy precious rich crown
for a pitiful bald crown.

FALSTAFF.   Well, and the fire of grace be not quite out of thee,
now shalt thou be moved. Give me a cup of sack to make
my eyes look red, that it may be thought I have wept; for   360
I must speak in passion, and I will do it in King Cambyses'
vein.°

---

334 **bluecaps** Scots
338-40 **if there . . . hundreds** (the Prince
applies the analogy of selling what won't
keep to the reactions of virgins as they
see all the men going off to war)
345 **spirit** i.e. evil spirit
346 **thrill** shiver (with fear)
353 **state** chair of state, i.e. throne

355 **taken for** (either "seen to be merely"; or, alternatively, this is a meditative
comment, possibly an aside, in the detached
vein of I ii 180ff and II iv 450, with "thy"
referring to the King)
361-62 **King . . . vein** i.e. the old rant-
ing style of Preston's *King Cambyses* (1569)

PRINCE.   Well, here is my leg.°

FALSTAFF.   And here is my speech. Stand aside, nobility.°

HOSTESS.   O Jesu, this is excellent sport, i' faith!   365

FALSTAFF.   Weep not, sweet queen,° for trickling tears are vain.

HOSTESS.   O, the Father, how he holds his countenance!°

FALSTAFF.   For God's sake, lords, convey my tristful° queen!
For tears do stop the floodgates of her eyes.

HOSTESS.   O Jesu, he doth it as like one of these harlotry°   370
players as ever I see!

FALSTAFF.   Peace, good pintpot. Peace, good tickle-brain.°
Harry, I do not only marvel where thou spendest thy time,
but also how thou art accompanied. For though the camomile,° the more it is trodden on, the faster it grows, so°   375
youth, the more it is wasted, the sooner it wears. That thou
art my son I have partly thy mother's word, partly my own
opinion, but chiefly a villainous trick° of thine eye and a
foolish hanging of thy nether° lip that doth warrant° me. If
then thou be son to me, here lies the point: why, being son   380
to me, art thou so pointed at? Shall the blessed son of
heaven prove a micher and eat blackberries?° A question
not to be asked. Shall the son° of England prove a thief
and take purses? A question to be asked. There is a thing,
Harry, which thou hast often heard of, and it is known to   385
many in our land by the name of pitch. This pitch (as
ancient writers do report) doth defile; so doth the company
thou keepest. For, Harry, now I do not speak to thee in
drink, but in tears; not in pleasure, but in passion; not in
words only, but in woes also: and yet there is a virtuous   390

---

363 **leg** i.e. bow (as if before the King)
364 **nobility** (addressed to his motley ra-
gamuffins)
366 **queen** (addressed to the Hostess, who
is evidently tearful with laughter, probably
with a standard pun on quean=tart, prosti-
tute)
367 **holds his countenance** keeps a
straight face
368 **tristful** sad
370 **harlotry** rascally
372 **Peace . . . tickle-brain** (Falstaff addresses the Hostess in terms suited to her
profession as server of alcoholic beverages)
374-75 **camomile** aromatic herb (Falstaff
proceeds to satirize the high-flown style
of the court by using a manner of speech

called euphuism—from John Lyly's fictional
narrative, *Euphues* [1578], which introduced
it—based on similies drawn from natural
history, intricate balance, antithesis, and
repetition of sounds, words, and ideas)
375 **so** (some editors emend to "yet,"
but the imperfect logical correspondence
of "though . . . so" may be part of Falstaff's mockery)
378 **trick** mannerism (possibly a twitch)
379 **nether** lower
379 **warrant** convince
382 **prove . . . blackberries** be a truant
from duty and go blackberrying
383 **son** (with pun on "sun," the royal
symbol)

man whom I have often noted in thy company, but I know
not his name.

PRINCE.   What manner of man, and it like your Majesty?

FALSTAFF.   A goodly portly° man, i' faith, and a corpulent;° of
a cheerful look, a pleasing eye, and a most noble carriage; 395
and, as I think, his age some fifty, or, by'r Lady, inclining
to threescore; and now I remember me, his name is Falstaff. If that man should be lewdly given,° he deceiveth
me; for, Harry, I see virtue in his looks. If then the tree
may be known by the fruit,° as the fruit by the tree, then, 400
peremptorily° I speak it, there is virtue in that Falstaff. Him
keep with, the rest banish. And tell me now, thou naughty
varlet, tell me where hast thou been this month?

PRINCE.   Dost thou speak like a king? Do thou stand for me,
and I'll play my father.   405

FALSTAFF.   Depose me? If thou dost it half so gravely, so
majestically, both in word and matter, hang me up by the
heels for a rabbit-sucker° or a poulter's hare.

PRINCE.   Well, here I am set.

FALSTAFF.   And here I stand. Judge, my masters.   410

PRINCE.   Now, Harry, whence come you?

FALSTAFF.   My noble lord, from Eastcheap.

PRINCE.   The complaints I hear of thee are grievous.

FALSTAFF.   'Sblood, my lord, they are false! Nay, I'll tickle ye
for a young prince,° i' faith.   415

PRINCE.   Swearest thou, ungracious boy? Henceforth ne'er
look on me. Thou art violently carried away from grace.
There is a devil haunts thee in the likeness of an old fat
man; a tun° of man is thy companion. Why dost thou con-
verse with that trunk of humors,° that bolting-hutch° of   420
beastliness, that swoll'n parcel of dropsies,° that huge

---

394 **portly** dignified
394 **corpulent** well filled out
398 **lewdly given** inclined to evil-doing
399-400 **If . . . fruit** (see Matthew 12:33:
"The tree is known by his fruit")
401 **peremptorily** decisively
408 **rabbit-sucker** suckling rabbit (again
an object long and thin)
414-15 **I'll . . . prince** I'll act a prince
that will amuse you

419 **tun** hogshead
420 **trunk of humors** receptacle of body
fluids (with allusion to the diseases that
were thought to be the product of these
fluids)
420 **bolting-hutch** sifting-bin (where im-
purities collect)
421 **dropsies** internal fluids

bombard° of sack, that stuffed cloakbag of guts, that
roasted Manningtree° ox with the pudding in his belly, that
reverend vice,° that gray iniquity,° that father ruffian,°
that vanity° in years? Wherein is he good, but to taste sack   425
and drink it? Wherein neat and cleanly, but to carve a
capon and eat it? Wherein cunning, but in craft?° Wherein
crafty, but in villainy? Wherein villainous, but in all
things? Wherein worthy, but in nothing?

FALSTAFF.   I would your Grace would take me with you.° Whom   430
means your Grace?

PRINCE.   That villainous abominable misleader of youth, Falstaff, that old white-bearded Satan.

FALSTAFF.   My lord, the man I know.

PRINCE.   I know thou dost.   435

FALSTAFF.   But to say I know more harm in him than in myself were to say more than I know. That he is old, the more
the pity, his white hairs do witness it; but that he is, sav-
ing your reverence, a whoremaster, that I utterly deny. If
sack and sugar be a fault, God help the wicked! If to be   440
old and merry be a sin, then many an old host that I know
is damned. If to be fat be to be hated, then Pharaoh's lean
kine° are to be loved. No, my good lord: banish Peto, banish Bardolph, banish Poins; but for sweet Jack Falstaff,
kind Jack Falstaff, true Jack Falstaff, valiant Jack Falstaff,   445
and therefore more valiant being, as he is, old Jack
Falstaff, banish not him thy Harry's company, banish not
him thy Harry's company, banish plump Jack, and banish
all the world!

PRINCE.   I do, I will. [*A knocking heard.*   450
                   Exeunt Hostess, Francis, and Bardolph.]
                Enter Bardolph, running.

BARDOLPH.   O, my lord, my lord! The sheriff with a most monstrous watch° is at the door.

---

422 bombard leather wine vessel
423 Manningtree town in Essex (where at
annual fairs plays were acted and, evidently,
great oxen were stuffed and barbecued)
424-25 vice, iniquity, ruffian, vanity (names
intended to associate Falstaff with characters of the old morality plays, all of whom
were corrupters of virtue, but who were

young, unlike Falstaff, who ought to know
better)
427 Wherein . . . craft i.e. wherein skill-
ful but in underhanded skills
430 take . . . you tell me what you're
talking about
443 kine cows (see Genesis 41:19-21)
452 watch group of constables

FALSTAFF.   Out, ye rogue! Play out the play, I have much to say in the behalf of that Falstaff.

Enter the Hostess.

HOSTESS.   O Jesu, my lord, my lord!   455

PRINCE.   Heigh, heigh, the devil rides upon a fiddlestick! What's the matter?

HOSTESS.   The sheriff and all the watch are at the door. They are come to search the house. Shall I let them in?

FALSTAFF.   Dost thou hear, Hal? Never call a true piece of gold   460 a counterfeit. Thou art essentially made without seeming so.°

PRINCE.   And thou a natural coward without instinct.

FALSTAFF.   I deny your major.° If you will deny the sheriff, so; if not, let him enter. If I become not a cart° as well as   465 another man, a plague on my bringing up! I hope I shall as soon be strangled with a halter as another.

PRINCE.   Go hide thee behind the arras.° The rest walk up above. Now, my masters, for a true face and good conscience.   470

FALSTAFF.   Both which I have had; but their date is out,° and therefore I'll hide me.   *Exit.*

PRINCE.   Call in the sheriff.

[Exeunt all but the Prince and Peto.]
Enter Sheriff and the Carrier.

Now, master sheriff, what is your will with me?

SHERIFF.   First, pardon me, my lord. A hue and cry   475 Hath followed certain men unto this house.

PRINCE.   What men?

SHERIFF.   One of them is well known, my gracious lord— A gross fat man.

CARRIER.   As fat as butter.   480

460-62 **Never . . . so** (a difficult passage, perhaps meaning that Falstaff, as a true piece of gold despite appearances, should not be turned over to the sheriff by a royal friend who is also true gold despite appearances)

464 **major** i.e. major premise (with pun on "mayor"—see "deny the sheriff" on the same line)
465 **cart** hangman's cart
468 **arras** wall-hanging
471 **date is out** term is over

PRINCE.   The man, I do assure you, is not here,
 For I myself at this time have employed him.°
 And, sheriff, I will engage° my word to thee
 That I will by tomorrow dinner time
 Send him to answer thee, or any man,   485
 For anything he shall be charged withal;°
 And so let me entreat you leave the house.

SHERIFF.   I will, my lord. There are two gentlemen
 Have in this robbery lost three hundred marks.

PRINCE.   It may be so. If he have robbed these men,   490
 He shall be answerable; and so farewell.

SHERIFF.   Good night, my noble lord.

PRINCE.   I think it is good morrow, is it not?

SHERIFF.   Indeed, my lord, I think it be two o'clock.

        Exit [with Carrier].

PRINCE.   This oily rascal is known as well as Paul's.° Go call   495
 him forth.

PETO.   Falstaff! Fast asleep behind the arras, and snorting°
 like a horse.

PRINCE.   Hark how hard he fetches breath. Search his pockets.
   He searcheth his pocket and findeth certain papers.
 What hast thou found?   500

PETO.   Nothing but papers, my lord.

PRINCE.   Let's see what they be. Read them.

[PETO *reads*]   "Item, A capon . . . . 2s. 2d.
   Item, Sauce . . . .   4d.
   Item, Sack two gallons 5s, 8d.   505
   Item, Anchovies and sack after supper   2s. 6d.
   Item, Bread . . . .   ob."°

PRINCE.   O monstrous! But one halfpennyworth of bread to this
 intolerable deal° of sack! What there is else, keep close;°
 we'll read it at more advantage. There let him sleep till day.   510

481-82 The man . . . him (Hal's reply is equivocal: Falstaff is not "here," in the heir-apparent's presence, but "employed" behind the arras)
483 engage pledge
486 withal with

495 Paul's St. Paul's church, a well-known building in London
497 snorting snoring
507 ob. obolus, halfpenny
509 deal lot
509 close i.e. private

I'll to the court in the morning. We must all to the wars,
and thy place shall be honorable. I'll procure this fat rogue
a charge of foot,° and I know his death will be a march of
twelve score.° The money shall be paid back again with
advantage.° Be with me betimes° in the morning, and so   515
good morrow, Peto.

PETO.   Good morrow, good my lord.   *Exeunt.*

Enter Hotspur, Worcester, Lord Mortimer,   *III i*
Owen Glendower.

MORTIMER.   These promises are fair, the parties sure,
And our induction° full of prosperous hope.

HOTSPUR.   Lord Mortimer, and cousin Glendower, will you sit
down? And uncle Worcester. A plague upon it! I have forgot the map.   5

GLENDOWER.   No, here it is. Sit, cousin Percy, sit, good cousin
Hotspur, for by that name as oft as Lancaster° doth speak
of you, his cheek looks pale, and with a rising sigh he
wisheth you in heaven.

HOTSPUR.   And you in hell, as oft as he hears Owen Glendower   10
spoke of.°

GLENDOWER.   I cannot blame him. At my nativity
The front of heaven was full of fiery shapes
Of burning cressets,° and at my birth
The frame and huge foundation of the earth   15
Shakèd like a coward.

HOTSPUR.   Why, so it would have done at the same season if
your mother's cat had but kittened, though yourself had
never been born.

---

513   **charge of foot** company of infantry
514   **twelve score** twelve score paces
515   **advantage** interest
515   **betimes** early
III i 2 **induction** beginning
7   **Lancaster** i.e. the King

3-11 **Lord . . . spoke of** (many editors
revise to read as verse, with line breaks
after   "down/it/is/Hotspur/you/sigh/hell/of"
or, leaving Hotspur's lines as prose, revise
Glendower's speech to read as verse with
breaks after "Percy/name/you/sigh/heaven")
14 **cressets** beacons

GLENDOWER.   I say the earth did shake when I was born.   20

HOTSPUR.   And I say the earth was not of my mind,
    If you suppose as fearing you it shook.

GLENDOWER.   The heavens were all on fire, the earth did
    tremble.

HOTSPUR.   O, then the earth shook to see the heavens on fire,
    And not in fear of your nativity.   25
    Diseasèd° nature oftentimes breaks forth
    In strange eruptions; oft the teeming earth
    Is with a kind of colic pinched and vexed
    By the imprisoning of unruly wind
    Within her womb, which, for enlargement° striving,   30
    Shakes the old beldame° earth and topples down
    Steeples and mossgrown towers. At your birth
    Our grandam earth, having this distemp'rature,°
    In passion° shook.

GLENDOWER.   Cousin, of many men   35
    I do not bear these crossings.° Give me leave
    To tell you once again that at my birth
    The front of heaven was full of fiery shapes,
    The goats ran from the mountains, and the herds
    Were strangely clamorous to the frighted fields.   40
    These signs have marked me extraordinary,
    And all the courses of my life do show
    I am not in the roll° of common men.
    Where is he living, clipped in with° the sea
    That chides the banks of England, Scotland, Wales,   45
    Which calls me pupil or hath read to° me?
    And bring him out that is but woman's son
    Can trace° me in the tedious ways of art°
    And hold me pace in deep experiments.

HOTSPUR.   I think there's no man speaks better Welsh.° I'll to   50
    dinner.

MORTIMER.   Peace, cousin Percy; you will make him mad.

<table>
<tr><td>26</td><td>Diseasèd disordered</td><td>43</td><td>roll register</td></tr>
<tr><td>30</td><td>enlargement escape</td><td>44</td><td>clipped in with embraced by</td></tr>
<tr><td>31</td><td>beldame grandmother (see "grandam,"</td><td>46</td><td>read to tutored</td></tr>
<tr><td></td><td>line 33)</td><td>48</td><td>trace follow</td></tr>
<tr><td>33</td><td>distemp'rature physical disorder</td><td>48</td><td>art magic</td></tr>
<tr><td>34</td><td>passion pain</td><td>50</td><td>speaks . . . Welsh (1) brags better (2)</td></tr>
<tr><td>36</td><td>crossings contradictions</td><td></td><td>talks more unintelligibly</td></tr>
</table>

GLENDOWER.   I can call spirits from the vasty deep.

HOTSPUR.   Why, so can I, or so can any man;
    But will they come when you do call for them?   55

GLENDOWER.   Why, I can teach you, cousin, to command the
    devil.

HOTSPUR.   And I can teach thee, coz, to shame the devil—
    By telling truth. Tell truth and shame the devil.
    If thou have power to raise him, bring him hither,   60
    And I'll be sworn I have power to shame him hence.
    O, while you live, tell truth and shame the devil!

MORTIMER.   Come, come, no more of this unprofitable chat.

GLENDOWER.   Three times hath Henry Bolingbroke made head°
    Against my power; thrice from the banks of Wye   65
    And sandy-bottomed Severn° have I sent him
    Booteless° home and weather-beaten back.

HOTSPUR.   Home without boots, and in foul weather too?
    How scapes he agues,° in the devil's name?

GLENDOWER.   Come, here is the map. Shall we divide our right°   70
    According to our threefold order° ta'en?

MORTIMER.   The Archdeacon hath divided it
    Into three limits° very equally.
    England, from Trent and Severn hitherto,°
    By south and east is to my part assigned;   75
    All westward, Wales beyond the Severn shore,
    And all the fertile land within that bound,
    To Owen Glendower; and, dear coz, to you
    The remnant northward lying off° from Trent.
    And our indentures tripartite° are drawn,   80
    Which being sealèd interchangeably°
    (A business that this night may execute),
    Tomorrow, cousin Percy, you and I
    And my good Lord of Worcester will set forth

---

64 made head raised an army
65-66 Wye, Severn rivers in west of England forming Welsh border
67 Booteless profitless (probably trisyllabic)
69 agues i.e. catching cold
70 our right i.e. the kingdom they hope to win
71 our . . . order agreement the three of us have made
73 limits regions
74 hitherto i.e. he points to a spot on the map before them
79 lying off starting
80 indentures tripartite three-way agreements
81 interchangeably i.e. by all three parties

To meet your father and the Scottish power,   85
As is appointed us, at Shrewsbury.
My father Glendower is not ready yet,
Nor shall we need his help these fourteen days.
[*To Glendower*] Within that space you may have drawn
    together
Your tenants, friends, and neighboring gentlemen.   90

GLENDOWER.   A shorter time shall send me to you, lords;
And in my conduct shall your ladies come,
From whom you now must steal and take no leave,
For there will be a world of water shed
Upon the parting of your wives and you.   95

HOTSPUR.   Methinks my moiety,° north from Burton here,
In quantity equals not one of yours.
See how this river comes me cranking° in
And cuts me from the best of all my land
A huge half-moon, a monstrous cantle° out.   100
I'll have the current in this place dammed up,
And here the smug° and silver Trent shall run
In a new channel fair and evenly.
It shall not wind with such a deep indent
To rob me of so rich a bottom° here.   105

GLENDOWER.   Not wind? It shall, it must! You see it doth.

MORTIMER.   Yea, but mark how he bears his course, and runs
me up with like advantage° on the other side, gelding the
opposèd continent° as much as on the other side it takes
from you.°   110

WORCESTER.   Yea, but a little charge° will trench° him here
And on this north side win this cape of land;
And then he runs straight and even.

HOTSPUR.   I'll have it so, a little charge will do it.

GLENDOWER.   I'll not have it alt'red.   115

HOTSPUR.   Will not you?

---

96 **moiety** share
98 **cranking** winding
100 **cantle** piece
102 **smug** smooth
105 **bottom** valley
108 **advantage** i.e. disadvantage

108-9 **gelding . . . continent** cutting out of the opposite bank
107-10 **Yea . . . you** (revised by many editors to read as verse, with breaks after "but/up/side/much/you")
111 **charge** cost
111 **trench** make a new course for

GLENDOWER.   No, nor you shall not.

HOTSPUR.   Who shall say me nay?

GLENDOWER.   Why, that will I.

HOTSPUR.   Let me not understand you then; speak it in Welsh.   120

GLENDOWER.   I can speak English, lord, as well as you;
　　　For I was trained up in the English court,
　　　Where, being but young, I framèd to the harp
　　　Many an English ditty lovely well,
　　　And gave the tongue a helpful ornament° —   125
　　　A virtue that was never seen in you.

HOTSPUR.   Marry, and I am glad of it with all my heart!
　　　I had rather be a kitten and cry mew
　　　Than one of these same meter ballad-mongers.°
　　　I had rather hear a brazen canstick turned°   130
　　　Or a dry wheel grate on the axletree,
　　　And that would set my teeth nothing on edge,
　　　Nothing so much as mincing° poetry.
　　　'Tis like the forced gait of a shuffling° nag.

GLENDOWER.   Come, you shall have Trent turned.   135

HOTSPUR.   I do not care. I'll give thrice so much land
　　　To any well-deserving friend;
　　　But in the way of bargain, mark ye me,
　　　I'll cavil on the ninth part of a hair.
　　　Are the indentures drawn? Shall we be gone?   140

GLENDOWER.   The moon shines fair; you may away by night.
　　　I'll haste the writer, and withal
　　　Break with° your wives of your departure hence.
　　　I am afraid my daughter will run mad,
　　　So much she doteth on her Mortimer.   *Exit.*   145

MORTIMER.   Fie, cousin Percy, how you cross my father!

HOTSPUR.   I cannot choose. Sometimes he angers me
　　　With telling me of the moldwarp° and the ant,
　　　Of the dreamer Merlin and his prophecies,

---

125 gave . . . ornament (1) ornamented
the words with music (?)　(2) benefited the
English language by my poems (?)
129 meter ballad-mongers singers of dog-
gerel ballads
130 canstick turned i.e. candlestick in
process of being burnished (and therefore
raucously scraped)

133 mincing affected
134 shuffling hobbled
143 Break with inform
148 moldwarp mole (i.e. Henry—see note
152)

And of a dragon and a finless fish,   150
A clip-winged griffin and a moulten raven,
A couching° lion and a ramping° cat,
And such a deal of skimble-skamble° stuff
As puts me from my faith. I tell you what—
He held me last night at least nine hours   155
In reckoning up the several devils' names
That were his lackeys. I cried "hum," and "Well, go to!"
But marked him not a word. O, he is as tedious
As a tired horse, a railing wife;
Worse than a smoky house. I had rather live   160
With cheese and garlic in a windmill far
Than feed on cates° and have him talk to me
In any summer house° in Christendom.

MORTIMER.   In faith, he is a worthy gentleman,
Exceedingly well read and profited   165
In strange concealments,° valiant as a lion,
And wondrous affable, and as bountiful
As mines of India. Shall I tell you, cousin?
He holds your temper in a high respect
And curbs himself even of his natural scope°   170
When you come 'cross his humor.° Faith, he does.
I warrant you that man is not alive
Might so have tempted° him as you have done
Without the taste of danger and reproof.
But do not use it oft, let me entreat you.   175

WORCESTER.   In faith, my lord, you are too willful-blame,°
And since your coming hither have done enough
To put him quite besides his patience.
You must needs learn, lord, to amend this fault.
Though sometimes it show greatness, courage, blood°—   180
And that's the dearest grace it renders you—
Yet oftentimes it doth present° harsh rage,

---

152 **couching, ramping** (Hotspur ridicules heraldic crouching and rearing beasts; evidently Glendower talked of ancient prophecies which held that the kingdom of the mole should be divided by the lion, dragon, and wolf, which were the crests of Percy, Glendower, and Mortimer)
153 **skimble-skamble** meaningless
162 **cates** delicacies
163 **summer house** country house

165-66 **profited . . . concealments** expert in secret arts
170 **scope** range of behavior
171 **come . . . humor** clash with his temperament
173 **tempted** provoked
176 **too willful-blame** blamable for too much willfulness
180 **blood** spirit
182 **present** indicate

Defect of manners, want of government,°
Pride, haughtiness, opinion,° and disdain;
The least of which haunting a nobleman   185
Loseth men's hearts, and leaves behind a stain
Upon the beauty of all parts besides,
Beguiling° them of commendation.

HOTSPUR.   Well, I am schooled. Good manners be your speed!°
Here come our wives, and let us take our leave.   190

Enter Glendower with the Ladies.

MORTIMER.   This is the deadly spite° that angers me—
My wife can speak no English, I no Welsh.

GLENDOWER.   My daughter weeps; she'll not part with you,
She'll be a soldier too, she'll to the wars.

MORTIMER.   Good father, tell her that she and my aunt Percy   195
Shall follow in your conduct speedily.

*Glendower speaks to her in Welsh, and
she answers him in the same.*

GLENDOWER.   She is desperate here.
A peevish self-willed harlotry,° one that no persuasion can
do good upon.   *The Lady speaks in Welsh.*

MORTIMER.   I understand thy looks. That pretty Welsh°   200
Which thou pourest down from these swelling heavens°
I am too perfect in; and, but for shame,
In such a parley° should I answer thee.
                              The Lady again in Welsh.
I understand thy kisses, and thou mine,
And that's a feeling disputation.°   205
But I will never be a truant, love,
Till I have learnt thy language; for thy tongue
Makes Welsh as sweet as ditties highly penned,°
Sung by a fair queen in a summer's bow'r,
With ravishing division,° to her lute.   210

---

183 **government** self-control
184 **opinion** arrogance
188 **Beguiling** depriving
189 **be your speed** bring you success
191 **spite** misfortune
198 **harlotry** ninny, fool
200 **That . . . Welsh** i.e. her tears

201 **heavens** i.e. her eyes
203 **parley** meeting (of tears)
205 **feeling disputation** dialogue by (1)
touching (2) the feelings
208 **highly penned** i.e. lofty
210 **division** musical variation

GLENDOWER.   Nay, if you melt,° then she will run mad.
The Lady speaks again in Welsh.

MORTIMER.   O, I am ignorance itself in this!

GLENDOWER.   She bids you on the wanton° rushes lay you down
And rest your gentle head upon her lap,
And she will sing the song that pleaseth you   215
And on your eyelids crown the god of sleep,°
Charming your blood with pleasing heaviness,
Making such difference 'twixt wake and sleep
As is the difference betwixt day and night
The hour before the heavenly-harnessed team°   220
Begins his golden progress in the east.

MORTIMER.   With all my heart I'll sit and hear her sing.
By that time will our book,° I think, be drawn.

GLENDOWER.   Do so, and those musicians that shall play to you
Hang in the air a thousand leagues from hence,   225
And straight they shall be here: sit, and attend.

HOTSPUR.   Come, Kate, thou art perfect in lying down.
Come, quick, quick, that I may lay my head in thy lap.

LADY PERCY.   Go, ye giddy goose.   *The music plays.*

HOTSPUR.   Now I perceive the devil understands Welsh,   230
And 'tis no marvel he is so humorous,°
By'r Lady, he is a good musician.

LADY PERCY.   Then should you be nothing but musical,
For you are altogether governed by humors.°
Lie still, ye thief, and hear the lady sing in Welsh.   235

HOTSPUR.   I had rather hear Lady, my brach,° howl in Irish.

LADY PERCY.   Wouldst thou have thy head broken?

HOTSPUR.   No.

LADY PERCY.   Then be still.

HOTSPUR.   Neither! 'Tis a woman's fault.   240

LADY PERCY.   Now God help thee!

---

211 **melt** weaken (i.e. by crying too)
213 **wanton** luxurious
216 **crown . . . sleep** i.e. give sleep sovereignty
220 **the . . . team** the horses of the sun

223 **book** agreement
231 **humorous** capricious
234 **humors** whims
236 **brach** bitch-hound

HOTSPUR.   To the Welsh lady's bed.

LADY PERCY.   What's that?

HOTSPUR.   Peace! She sings.

                                 Here the Lady sings a Welsh song.

    Come, Kate, I'll have your song too.   245

LADY PERCY.   Not mine, in good sooth.°

HOTSPUR.   Not yours, in good sooth? Heart, you swear like a
    comfit-maker's° wife. "Not you, in good sooth!" and "as true
    as I live!" and "as God shall mend me!" and "as sure as day!"
    And givest such sarcenet surety° for thy oaths   250
    As if thou never walk'st further than Finsbury.°
    Swear me, Kate, like a lady as thou art,
    A good mouth-filling oath, and leave "in sooth"
    And such protest of pepper gingerbread°
    To velvet guards° and Sunday citizens.   255
    Come, sing.

LADY PERCY.   I will not sing.

HOTSPUR.   'Tis the next way to turn tailor° or be redbreast-
    teacher.° And the indentures be drawn, I'll away within
    these two hours; and so come in when ye will.   *Exit.* 260

GLENDOWER.   Come, come, Lord Mortimer. You are as slow
    As hot Lord Percy is on fire to go.
    By this our book is drawn; we'll but seal,
    And then to horse immediately.

MORTIMER.   With all my heart.   *Exeunt.* 265

                                  ~∞~✕~∞~

         Enter the King, Prince of Wales, and others.   **III**

KING.   Lords, give us leave: the Prince of Wales and I
    Must have some private conference; but be near at hand,
    For we shall presently have need of you.   *Exeunt Lords.*

---

246 **sooth** truth
248 **comfit-maker's** confectioner's
250 **sarcenet surety** flimsy security ("sarcenet"—a thin silk)
251 **Finsbury** resort near London (fre-
quented by the Puritan middle-class groups
whose distaste for swearing Hotspur sati-
rizes)

254 **pepper gingerbread** i.e. insubstantial,
crumbling in the mouth
255 **velvet guards** i.e. shopkeepers, who
favored velvet trimmings for Sunday wear
258 **tailor** (like weavers, tailors were
famed for singing at their work)
258-59 **redbreast-teacher** singing master to
songbirds

I know not whether God will have it so
For some displeasing service I have done,   5
That, in his secret doom,° out of my blood°
He'll breed revengement and a scourge for me;
But thou dost in thy passages° of life
Make me believe that thou art only marked
For the hot vengeance and the rod of heaven   10
To punish my mistreadings.° Tell me else,
Could such inordinate° and low desires,
Such poor, such bare, such lewd,° such mean attempts,°
Such barren pleasures, rude society,
As thou art matched withal° and grafted to,   15
Accompany the greatness of thy blood
And hold their level with thy princely heart?

PRINCE.   So please your Majesty, I would I could
Quit° all offenses with as clear excuse
As well° as I am doubtless° I can purge   20
Myself of many I am charged withal.
Yet such extenuation let me beg
As, in reproof of many tales devised,
Which oft the ear of greatness needs must hear
By smiling pickthanks and base newsmongers,   25
I may, for some things true wherein my youth
Hath faulty wand'red and irregular,
Find pardon on my true submission.°

KING.   God pardon thee! Yet let me wonder, Harry,
At thy affections,° which do hold a wing   30
Quite from° the flight of all thy ancestors.
Thy place in council thou hast rudely lost,
Which by thy younger brother is supplied,
And art almost an alien to the hearts
Of all the court and princes of my blood.   35

III ii 6 **doom** judgment
6 **blood** i.e. heirs
8 **passages** courses
9-11 thou . . . mistreadings i.e. (1) heaven is punishing me through you (2) heaven will punish you to punish me
12 inordinate i.e. out of order (for one of your rank)
13 lewd ignorant
13 attempts action
15 withal with
19 Quit clear myself of

20 As well and as well
20 am doubtless have no doubt
22-28 Yet . . . submission yet let me beg such extenuation that when I have confuted many manufactured charges (which the ear of greatness is bound to hear from informers and tattletales) I may be pardoned for some true faults of which my youth has been guilty
30 affections tastes
31 Quite from quite opposite from

The hope and expectation of thy time°
Is ruined, and the soul of every man
Prophetically do forethink thy fall.
Had I so lavish of my presence been,
So common-hackneyed° in the eyes of men,   40
So stale and cheap to vulgar company,
Opinion,° that did help me to the crown,
Had still kept loyal to possession°
And left me in reputeless banishment,
A fellow of no mark nor likelihood.   45
By being seldom seen, I could not stir
But, like a comet, I was wond'red at;
That men would tell their children, "This is he!"
Others would say, "Where? Which is Bolingbroke?"
And then I stole all courtesy from heaven,°   50
And dressed myself in such humility
That I did pluck allegiance from men's hearts,
Loud shouts and salutations from their mouths
Even in the presence of the crownèd King.
Thus did I keep my person fresh and new,   55
My presence, like a robe pontifical,
Ne'er seen but wond'red at; and so my state,°
Seldom but sumptuous, showed like a feast
And won by rareness such solemnity.
The skipping King, he ambled up and down   60
With shallow jesters and rash bavin° wits,
Soon kindled and soon burnt; carded° his state;
Mingled his royalty with cap'ring fools;
Had his great name profanèd with their scorns
And gave his countenance, against his name,°   65
To laugh at gibing boys and stand the push°
Of every beardless vain comparative;°
Grew a companion to the common streets,

---

36 **time** reign
40 **common-hackneyed** cheapened
42 **Opinion** public opinion
43 **possession** i.e. Richard II
50 **I . . . heaven** I took a godlike graciousness on myself
57 **state** dignified behavior
60-67 **The . . . comparative** (Henry stresses the immaturity of Richard's adolescent tastes and companions whom he allowed to be too free with him)

61 **bavin** brushwood (which flares and burns out)
62 **carded** debased
65 **his name** i.e. (1) his kingly title (2) his kingly authority
66 **stand the push** put up with the impudence
67 **comparative** deviser of insulting comparisons

Enfeoffed himself to popularity;°
That, being daily swallowed by men's eyes,   70
They surfeited° with honey and began
To loathe the taste of sweetness, whereof a little
More than a little is by much too much.
So, when he had occasion to be seen,
He was but as the cuckoo is in June,   75
Heard, not regarded—seen, but with such eyes
As, sick and blunted with community,°
Afford no extraordinary gaze,
Such as is bent on sunlike majesty
When it shines seldom in admiring eyes;   80
But rather drowsed and hung their eyelids down,
Slept in his face, and rend'red such aspect
As cloudy° men use to their adversaries,
Being with his presence glutted, gorged, and full.
And in that very line, Harry, standest thou;   85
For thou hast lost thy princely privilege
With vile participation.° Not an eye
But is aweary of thy common sight,
Save mine, which hath desired to see thee more;
Which now doth that I would not have it do—   90
Make blind itself with foolish tenderness.°

PRINCE.   I shall hereafter, my thrice-gracious lord,
Be more myself.

KING.   For all the world,
As thou art to this hour was Richard then   95
When I from France set foot at Ravenspurgh;
And even as I was then is Percy now.
Now, by my scepter, and my soul to boot,
He hath more worthy interest° to the state
Than thou the shadow of succession;   100
For of no right, nor color° like to right,
He doth fill fields with harness° in the realm,

---

69 **Enfeoffed . . . popularity** bound himself to low company
71 **surfeited** overstuffed (themselves)
77 **with community** by familiarity (with the king)
83 **cloudy** sullen (but also with reference to "clouds" obscuring the royal "sun")

87 **vile participation** companionship with low characters
91 **tenderness** i.e. tears
99 **worthy interest** claim based on worth (as compared with a "shadow" claim by inheritance)
101 **color** pretense
102 **harness** armor

Turns head° against the lion's° armèd jaws,
And, being no more in debt to years than thou,
Leads ancient lords and reverend bishops on   105
To bloody battles and to bruising arms.
What never-dying honor hath he got
Against renownèd Douglas! whose high deeds,
Whose hot incursions and great name in arms
Holds from all soldiers chief majority°   110
And military title capital°
Through all the kingdoms that acknowledge Christ.
Thrice hath this Hotspur, Mars in swathling clothes,
This infant warrior, in his enterprises
Discomfited° great Douglas; ta'en him once,   115
Enlargèd° him, and made a friend of him,
To fill the mouth of deep defiance up°
And shake the peace and safety of our throne.
And what say you to this? Percy, Northumberland,
The Archbishop's grace of York, Douglas, Mortimer   120
Capitulate° against us and are up.°
But wherefore do I tell these news to thee?
Why, Harry, do I tell thee of my foes,
Which are my nearest and dearest° enemy?
Thou that are like enough, through vassal fear,   125
Base inclination, and the start of spleen,
To fight against me under Percy's pay,
To dog his heels and curtsy at his frowns,
To show how much thou art degenerate.

PRINCE.   Do not think so, you shall not find it so.   130
And God forgive them that so much have swayed
Your Majesty's good thoughts away from me.
I will redeem all this on Percy's head
And, in the closing of some glorious day,
Be bold to tell you that I am your son,   135
When I will wear a garment all of blood,
And stain my favors° in a bloody mask,

---

103 **head** an army
103 **the lion's** i.e. the King's
110 **majority** preeminence
111 **capital** topmost
115 **Discomfited** defeated
116 **Enlargèd** set free
117 **To fill . . . up** to deepen the noise
of defiance

121 **Capitulate** (1) make a "head" or
armed force (?) (2) draw up "heads" of
an argument (?)
121 **up** in arms
124 **dearest** (1) most loved (2) costliest
137 **favors** features

Which, washed away, shall scour my shame° with it.
And that shall be the day, whene'er it lights,
That this same child of honor and renown,   140
This gallant Hotspur, this all-praisèd knight,
And your unthought-of Harry chance to meet.
For every honor sitting on his helm,
Would they were multitudes, and on my head
My shames redoubled! For the time will come   145
That I shall make this northern youth exchange
His glorious deeds for my indignities.
Percy is but my factor,° good my lord,
To engross° up glorious deeds on my behalf;
And I will call him to so strict account   150
That he shall render every glory up,
Yea, even the slightest worship of his time,°
Or I will tear the reckoning from his heart.
This in the name of God I promise here;
The which if he be pleased I shall perform,   155
I do beseech your Majesty may salve
The long-grown° wounds of my intemperance.°
If not, the end of life cancels all bands,°
And I will die a hundred thousand deaths
Ere break the smallest parcel° of this vow.   160

KING. A hundred thousand rebels die in this!
    Thou shalt have charge° and sovereign trust herein.

                    Enter Blunt.

How now, good Blunt? Thy looks are full of speed.

BLUNT. So hath the business° that I come to speak of.
    Lord Mortimer of Scotland hath sent word   165
    That Douglas and the English rebels met
    The eleventh of this month at Shrewsbury.
    A mighty and a fearful head they are,
    If promises be kept on every hand,
    As ever off'red foul play in a state.   170

---

138 **shame** disgrace
148 **factor** agent
149 **engross** hoard
152 **worship . . . time** honor he has
gained in his lifetime
157 **long-grown** old

157 **intemperance** riotous behavior
158 **bands** bonds, promises
160 **parcel** item
162 **charge** command
164 **So . . . business** i.e. the business
too has speed (must be dealt with speedily)

KING.   The Earl of Westmoreland set forth today;
With him my son, Lord John of Lancaster:
For this advertisement° is five days old.
On Wednesday next, Harry, you shall set forward;
On Thursday we ourselves will march. Our meeting   175
Is Bridgenorth; and, Harry, you shall march
Through Gloucestershire; by which account
Our business valuèd,° some twelve days hence
Our general forces at Bridgenorth shall meet.
Our hands are full of business. Let's away: 180
Advantage feeds him° fat while men delay.   *Exeunt.*

Enter Falstaff and Bardolph.   III iii

FALSTAFF.   Bardolph, am I not fall'n away vilely since this last
action?° Do I not bate?° Do I not dwindle? Why, my skin
hangs about me like an old lady's loose gown! I am
withered like an old apple-john.° Well, I'll repent, and that
suddenly,° while I am in some liking.° I shall be out of   5
heart° shortly, and then I shall have no strength to repent.
And I have not forgotten what the inside of a church is
made of, I am a peppercorn,° a brewer's horse.° The inside
of a church! Company, villainous company, hath been the
spoil° of me.   10

BARDOLPH.   Sir John, you are so fretful you cannot live long.

FALSTAFF.   Why, there is it! Come, sing me a bawdy song, make
me merry. I was as virtuously given as a gentleman need
to be, virtuous enough: swore little, diced not above seven
times a week, went to a bawdy house not above once in a   15
quarter of an hour, paid money that I borrowed three or

---

173 **advertisement** information
178 **Our . . . valuèd** having sized up
what we have to do
181 **him** itself
III iii 2 **action** i.e. the robbery
2 **bate** lose weight
4 **old apple-john** apple with shriveled
skin
5 **suddenly** right away

5 **am . . . liking** (1) am in the mood
(2) still have some flesh left
5-6 **out of heart** (1) out of the mood
(2) out of shape
8 **peppercorn, brewer's horse** (Falstaff
this time picks things not long and thin,
but dry, withered, decrepit)
10 **spoil** ruin

four times,° lived well, and in good compass;° and now I
live out of all order, out of all compass.

BARDOLPH.   Why, you are so fat, Sir John, that you must needs
be out of all compass—out of all reasonable compass, Sir   20
John.

FALSTAFF.   Do thou amend thy face,° and I'll amend my life.
Thou art our admiral,° thou bearest the lantern in the poop
—but 'tis in the nose of thee: thou art the Knight of the
Burning Lamp.   25

BARDOLPH.   Why, Sir John, my face does you no harm.

FALSTAFF.   No, I'll be sworn. I make as good use of it as many
a man doth of a death's-head° or a memento mori.° I
never see thy face but I think upon hellfire and Dives° that
lived in purple; for there he is in his robes, burning, burn-   30
ing. If thou wert any way given to virtue, I would swear
by thy face; my oath should be "By this fire, that's God's
angel."° But thou art altogether given over,° and wert
indeed, but for the light in thy face, the son of utter darkness. When thou ran'st up Gad's Hill in the night to catch   35
my horse, if I did not think thou hadst been an ignis
fatuus° or a ball of wildfire,° there's no purchase in money.
O, thou art a perpetual triumph,° an everlasting bonfire-
light! Thou hast saved me a thousand marks in links° and
torches, walking with thee in the night betwixt tavern and   40
tavern; but the sack that thou hast drunk me would have
bought me lights as good cheap° at the dearest chandler's°
in Europe. I have maintained that salamander° of yours
with fire any time this two and thirty years. God reward
me for it!   45

14-17 **diced . . . times** (probably spoken
with significant pauses after "diced not,"
"once," "borrowed")
17 **compass** order (but Bardolph takes it
in the sense of "size")
22 **face** (which is blotched and ruddy—
see II iv 290-4)
23 **admiral** flagship (recognizable by its
lantern)
28 **death's-head** ring with a skull
28 **memento mori** reminder of death
29 **Dives** uncharitable rich man who
burns in hell (Luke 16:19-31)
33 **angel** (alluding to the Scriptural ac-
counts of angels manifesting themselves as
fire, or possibly to the seraphs, highest
order of angels, who were fire)
33 **given over** committed to the Devil
36-37 **ignis fatuus** will-o'-wisp
37 **ball of wildfire** firework
38 **triumph** i.e. of the Roman kind, with
torches
39 **links** flares
42 **good cheap** cheaply
42 **dearest chandler's** most expensive
candle maker's
43 **salamander** lizard supposed to live in
fire

BARDOLPH.   'Sblood, I would my face were in your belly!°

FALSTAFF.   God-a-mercy! So should I be sure to be heart-burned.

Enter Hostess.

How now, Dame Partlet° the hen? Have you enquired yet
who picked my pocket?   50

HOSTESS.   Why, Sir John, what do you think, Sir John? Do you
think I keep thieves in my house? I have searched, I have
enquired, so has my husband, man by man, boy by boy,
servant by servant. The tithe° of a hair was never lost in
my house before.   55

FALSTAFF.   Ye lie, hostess. Bardolph was shaved and lost many
a hair, and I'll be sworn my pocket was picked. Go to, you
are a woman,° go!

HOSTESS.   Who, I? No;° I defy thee! God's light, I was never
called so in mine own house before!   60

FALSTAFF.   Go to, I know you well enough.

HOSTESS.   No, Sir John; you do not know me, Sir John. I know
you, Sir John. You owe me money, Sir John, and now you
pick a quarrel to beguile° me of it. I bought you a dozen of
shirts to your back.   65

FALSTAFF.   Dowlas,° filthy dowlas! I have given them away to
bakers' wives; they have made bolters° of them.

HOSTESS.   Now, as I am a true woman, holland° of eight shillings an ell.° You owe money here besides, Sir John, for
your diet and by-drinkings,° and money lent you, four and   70
twenty pound.

FALSTAFF.   He had his part of it: let him pay.

HOSTESS.   He? Alas, he is poor; he hath nothing.

FALSTAFF.   How? Poor? Look upon his face. What call you

---

46 **I . . . belly** (proverbial retort, to
which Falstaff's reply gives new life)
49 **Dame Partlet** (traditional name for a
hen, and well-suited to the clucking
Hostess)
54 **tithe** tenth part
58 **woman** i.e. a lewd woman, a bawd
59 **No** (the Hostess suspects that any
word or phrase of Falstaff's may contain
hidden innuendoes about her moral char-

acter; she sometimes retorts with comments containing amusing innuendoes about
herself that she is too ignorant to understand)
64 **beguile** cheat
66 **Dowlas** coarse linen
67 **bolters** sieves
68 **holland** fine linen
69 **ell** one and a quarter yards
70 **by-drinkings** drinks between meals

rich?° Let them coin his nose, let them coin his cheeks. 75
I'll not pay a denier.° What, will you make a younker° of
me? Shall I not take mine ease in mine inn but I shall
have my pocket picked? I have lost a seal ring of my
grandfather's worth forty mark.

HOSTESS.   O Jesu, I have heard the Prince tell him, I know not 80
how oft, that that ring was copper!

FALSTAFF.   How? The Prince is a Jack,° a sneak-up.° 'Sblood,
and he were here, I would cudgel° him like a dog if he
would say so.

Enter the Prince [and Poins], marching, and Falstaff
meets them, playing upon his truncheon° like a fife.

How now, lad? Is the wind in that door,° i' faith? Must we 85
all march?

BARDOLPH.   Yea, two and two,° Newgate fashion.

HOSTESS.   My lord, I pray you hear me.

PRINCE.   What say'st thou, Mistress Quickly? How doth thy
husband? I love him well, he is an honest man.   90

HOSTESS.   Good my lord, hear me.

FALSTAFF.   Prithee let her alone and list to me.

PRINCE.   What say'st thou, Jack?

FALSTAFF.   The other night I fell asleep here behind the arras
and had my pocket picked. This house is turned bawdy 95
house; they pick pockets.

PRINCE.   What didst thou lose, Jack?

FALSTAFF.   Wilt thou believe me, Hal, three or four bonds of
forty pound apiece and a seal ring of my grandfather's.

PRINCE.   A trifle, some eightpenny matter.   100

HOSTESS.   So I told him, my lord, and I said I heard your Grace
say so; and, my lord, he speaks most vilely of you, like a
foulmouthed man as he is, and said he would cudgel you.

---

75 **rich** (referring to its red gold-and-copper hues)
76 **denier** tenth of a penny
76 **younker** greenhorn
82 **Jack** rascal
82 **sneak-up** sneak

83 **cudgel** beat with a short stick (a cudgel)
84 **s.d. truncheon** cudgel
85 **Is . . . door** i.e. is that how things are going
87 **two and two** i.e. bound in pairs like prisoners on the way to (Newgate) prison

PRINCE.   What! He did not?

HOSTESS.   There's neither faith, truth, nor womanhood in me 105
else.

FALSTAFF.   There's no more faith in thee than in a stewed
prune,° nor no more truth in thee than in a drawn° fox;
and for womanhood, Maid Marian may be the deputy's
wife of the ward to thee.° Go, you thing, go!   110

HOSTESS.   Say, what thing, what thing?

FALSTAFF.   What thing? Why, a thing to thank God on.

HOSTESS.   I am no thing to thank God on, I would thou
shouldst know it! I am an honest man's wife, and, setting
thy knighthood aside, thou art a knave to call me so.   115

FALSTAFF.   Setting thy womanhood aside, thou art a beast to
say otherwise.

HOSTESS.   Say, what beast, thou knave, thou?

FALSTAFF.   What beast? Why, an otter.

PRINCE.   An otter, Sir John? Why an otter?   120

FALSTAFF.   Why, she's neither fish nor flesh; a man knows not
where to have her.°

HOSTESS.   Thou art an unjust man in saying so. Thou or any
man knows where to have me, thou knave, thou!

PRINCE.   Thou say'st true, hostess, and he slanders thee most 125
grossly.

HOSTESS.   So he doth you, my lord, and said this other day you
ought° him a thousand pound.

PRINCE.   Sirrah, do I owe you a thousand pound?

FALSTAFF.   A thousand pound, Hal? A million! Thy love is 130
worth a million, thou owest me thy love.

HOSTESS.   Nay, my lord, he called you Jack and said he would
cudgel you.

107-8 **stewed prune** (evidently chosen by
Falstaff because stewed prunes were asso-
ciated with bawdy houses)
108 **drawn** drawn from his lair and trying every trick to get back to it
109-10 **Maid . . . thee** a disreputable
female in country May games is chaste as
the wife of the ward's most respectable
citizen in comparison with you
122 **where . . . her** (Falstaff means "how
to deal with her," but again her reply
[123-24] assumes another meaning)
128 **ought** owed

FALSTAFF. Did I, Bardolph?

BARDOLPH. Indeed, Sir John, you said so.   135

FALSTAFF. Yea, if he said my ring was copper.

PRINCE. I say 'tis copper. Darest thou be as good as thy word now?

FALSTAFF. Why, Hal, thou knowest, as thou art but man, I dare; but as thou art Prince, I fear thee as I fear the roar-   140 ing of the lion's whelp.

PRINCE. And why not as the lion?

FALSTAFF. The King himself is to be feared as the lion. Dost thou think I'll fear thee as I fear thy father? Nay, and I do, I pray God my girdle° break.   145

PRINCE. O, if it should, how would thy guts fall about thy knees! But, sirrah, there's no room for faith, truth, nor honesty in this bosom of thine. It is all filled up with guts and midriff. Charge an honest woman with picking thy pocket? Why, thou whoreson, impudent, embossed° rascal,°   150 if there were anything in thy pocket but tavern reckonings, memorandums of bawdy houses, and one poor pennyworth of sugar candy to make thee long-winded—if thy pocket were enriched with any other injuries° but these, I am a villain. And yet you will stand to it;° you will not pocket   155 up° wrong. Art thou not ashamed?

FALSTAFF. Dost thou hear, Hal? Thou knowest in the state of innocency Adam fell, and what should poor Jack Falstaff do in the days of villainy? Thou seest I have more flesh than another man, and therefore more frailty. You confess   160 then, you picked my pocket?

PRINCE. It appears so by the story.

FALSTAFF. Hostess, I forgive thee, go make ready breakfast, love thy husband, look to thy servants, cherish thy guests. Thou shalt find me tractable to any honest reason. Thou   165 seest I am pacified still. Nay, prithee be gone.

                                                Exit Hostess.

---

145 girdle sword belt
150 embossed (1) swollen (2) foaming at the mouth (of a deer)
150 rascal (1) rogue (2) lean young deer

154 injuries i.e. things whose loss you call injuries
155 stand to it press your claim (against the Hostess)
155-56 pocket up peaceably put up with

Now, Hal, to the news at court. For the robbery, lad—how
is that answered?

PRINCE. O my sweet beef, I must still be good angel to thee.
The money is paid back again.   170

FALSTAFF. O, I do not like that paying back! 'Tis a double
labor.

PRINCE. I am good friends with my father, and may do anything.

FALSTAFF. Rob me the exchequer the first thing thou doest,   175
and do it with unwashed hands° too.

BARDOLPH. Do, my lord.

PRINCE. I have procured thee, Jack, a charge of foot.°

FALSTAFF. I would it had been of horse. Where shall I find one
that can steal well?° O for a fine thief of the age of two   180
and twenty or thereabouts! I am heinously unprovided.°
Well, God be thanked for these rebels, they offend none
but the virtuous: I laud them, I praise them.

PRINCE. Bardolph!

BARDOLPH. My lord?   185

PRINCE. Go bear this letter to Lord John of Lancaster,
To my brother John; this to my Lord of Westmoreland.
                              [*Exit Bardolph.*]
Go, Peto, to horse, to horse; for thou and I
Have thirty miles to ride yet ere dinner time.   [*Exit Peto.*]
Jack, meet me tomorrow in the Temple Hall   190
At two o'clock in the afternoon.
There shalt thou know thy charge,° and there receive
Money and order for their furniture.°
The land is burning, Percy stands on high,
And either we or they must lower lie.   [*Exit.*]   195

FALSTAFF. Rare words! Brave world! Hostess, my breakfast,
come.
O, I could wish this tavern were my drum!°   [*Exit.*]

---

176 **with . . . hands** with no delay
178 **charge of foot** command of foot
soldiers
180 **steal well** i.e. steal a horse for me
(among other things)

181 **heinously unprovided** wickedly un-
supplied
192 **thy charge** the command to be assigned to you
193 **furniture** equipment
197 **drum** recruiting center

~~~

[*Enter Hotspur, Worcester, and Douglas.*]   IV i

HOTSPUR.   Well said, my noble Scot. If speaking truth
     In this fine° age were not thought flattery,
     Such attribution° should the Douglas have
     As not a soldier of this season's stamp
     Should go so general current° through the world.   5
     By God, I cannot flatter, I do defy°
     The tongues of soothers!° But a braver place
     In my heart's love hath no man than yourself.
     Nay, task me to my word; approve me,° lord.

DOUGLAS.   Thou art the king of honor.   10
     No man so potent breathes upon the ground
     But I will beard° him.

                    Enter one with letters.

HOTSPUR.   Do so, and 'tis well.—
     What letters hast thou there?—I can but thank you.

MESSENGER.   These letters come from your father.   15

HOTSPUR.   Letters from him? Why comes he not himself?

MESSENGER.   He cannot come, my lord, he is grievous sick.

HOTSPUR.   Zounds! How has he the leisure to be sick
     In such a justling° time? Who leads his power?
     Under whose government° come they along?   20

MESSENGER.   His letters bears° his mind, not I, my lord.

WORCESTER.   I prithee tell me, doth he keep his bed?

MESSENGER.   He did, my lord, four days ere I set forth,
     And at the time of my departure thence
     He was much feared° by his physicians.   25

IV i 2 **fine** overly subtle
3 **attribution** recognition
5 **go . . . current** be as widely accepted
(the image is of a coin of recent mintage:
"this season's stamp")
6 **defy** despise
7 **soothers** flatterers
9 **task me . . . approve me** try me, test
me

12 **beard** oppose
19 **justling** jostling, unquiet
20 **government** command
21 **bears** (a singular verb with plural
subject is not uncommon in Elizabethan
English)
25 **feared** feared for

WORCESTER.   I would the state of time had first been whole
          Ere he by sickness had been visited.
          His health was never better worth than now.

HOTSPUR.   Sick now? Droop now? This sickness doth infect
          The very lifeblood of our enterprise.   30
          'Tis catching hither, even to our camp.
          He writes me here that inward sickness—
          And that his friends by deputation°
          Could not so soon be drawn; nor did he think it meet
          To lay so dangerous and dear a trust   35
          On any soul removed but on his own.
          Yet doth he give us bold advertisement,°
          That with our small conjunction° we should on,
          To see how fortune is disposed to us;
          For, as he writes, there is no quailing° now,   40
          Because the King is certainly possessed°
          Of all our purposes. What say you to it?

WORCESTER.   Your father's sickness is a maim to us.

HOTSPUR.   A perilous gash, a very limb lopped off.
          And yet, in faith, it is not! His present want°   45
          Seems more than we shall find it. Were it good
          To set° the exact wealth of all our states
          All at one cast? To set so rich a main°
          On the nice hazard° of one doubtful hour?
          It were not good; for therein should we read   50
          The very bottom and the soul° of hope,
          The very list,° the very utmost bound
          Of all our fortunes.

DOUGLAS.   Faith, and so we should.
          Where now remains a sweet reversion,°   55
          We may boldly spend upon the hope of what is to come in.
          A comfort of retirement° lives in this.

---

33 **deputation** a deputy
37 **advertisement** warning
38 **conjunction** combination of forces
40 **quailing** shrinking back
41 **possessed** informed
45 **want** loss
47 **set** risk
48 **main** (1) stake (in gambling) (2) army

49 **nice hazard** dangerous chance (continuing the dicing image)
51 **soul** (1) essence (2) sole (see "bottom")
52 **list** limit
55 **reversion** inheritance still to be received
57 **A . . . retirement** a security to fall back on

HOTSPUR.　A rendezvous, a home to fly unto,
　　If that the devil and mischance look big°
　　Upon the maidenhead° of our affairs.　　　　　　　60

WORCESTER.　But yet I would your father had been here.
　　The quality and hair° of our attempt
　　Brooks° no division. It will be thought
　　By some that know not why he is away,
　　That wisdom, loyalty, and mere dislike　　　　　　65
　　Of our proceedings kept the Earl from hence.
　　And think how such an apprehension°
　　May turn the tide of fearful faction°
　　And breed a kind of question in° our cause.
　　For well you know we of the off'ring side°　　　　70
　　Must keep aloof from strict arbitrement,°
　　And stop all sight-holes, every loop° from whence
　　The eye of reason may pry in upon us.
　　This absence of your father's draws° a curtain
　　That shows the ignorant a kind of fear　　　　　　75
　　Before not dreamt of.

HOTSPUR.　You strain too far.
　　I rather of his absence make this use:
　　It lends a luster and more great opinion,°
　　A larger dare to our great enterprise,　　　　　　80
　　Than if the Earl were here; for men must think,
　　If we, without his help, can make a head°
　　To push against a kingdom, with his help
　　We shall o'erturn it topsy-turvy down.
　　Yet all goes well; yet all our joints are whole.　　85

DOUGLAS.　As heart can think. There is not such a word
　　Spoke of in Scotland as this term of fear.

　　　　　　　Enter Sir Richard Vernon.

HOTSPUR.　My cousin Vernon, welcome, by my soul.

---

59 big menacingly
60 maidenhead forepart
62 hair nature
63 Brooks allows of
67 apprehension interpretation
68 May . . . faction may change the minds of any timid supporters
69 question in doubt about

70 we . . . side we who take the offensive
71 strict arbitrement close evaluation
72 loop loophole
74 draws draws aside
79 opinion prestige
82 a head (1) an army (2) headway

VERNON.   Pray God my news be worth a welcome, lord.
          The Earl of Westmoreland, seven thousand strong,   90
          Is marching hitherwards; with him Prince John.

HOTSPUR.   No harm. What more?

VERNON.   And further, I have learned
          The King himself in person is set forth,
          Or hitherwards intended speedily,   95
          With strong and mighty preparation.

HOTSPUR.   He shall be welcome too. Where is his son,
          The nimble-footed madcap Prince of Wales,
          And his comrades, that daffed° the world aside
          And bid it pass?   100

VERNON.   All furnished, all in arms;
          All plumed like estridges° that with the wind
          Bated° like eagles having lately bathed;
          Glittering in golden coats like images;
          As full of spirit as the month of May   105
          And gorgeous as the sun in midsummer;
          Wanton° as youthful goats, wild as young bulls.
          I saw young Harry with his beaver° on,
          His cushes° on his thighs, gallantly armed,
          Rise from the ground like feathered Mercury,°   110
          And vaulted with such ease into his seat
          As if an angel dropped down from the clouds
          To turn and wind a fiery Pegasus°
          And witch° the world with noble horsemanship.

HOTSPUR.   No more, no more! Worse than the sun in March,   115
          This praise doth nourish agues.° Let them come.
          They come like sacrifices in their trim,°
          And to the fire-eyed maid° of smoky war
          All hot and bleeding will we offer them.

---

99 **daffed** thrust
102 **estridges** ostriches (ostrich plumes are the emblem of the Prince of Wales)
103 **Bated** shook their wings
107 **Wanton** exuberant
108 **beaver** helmet
109 **cushes** thigh armor
110 **feathered Mercury** (the gods' messenger Mercury is normally depicted with winged sandals)
113 **To . . . Pegasus** ("turn" and "wind" are horsemanship terms, the latter mean-ing "wheel about"; Pegasus is the mythological winged horse; here the reference is to a very spirited horse that the Prince handles with great skill)
114 **witch** bewitch
116 **agues** chills and fever (the spring sun was believed to set them going)
117 **trim** trimmings
118 **maid** Bellona, goddess of war

The mailèd Mars° shall on his altars sit   120
Up to the ears in blood. I am on fire
To hear this rich reprisal° is so nigh,
And yet not ours. Come, let me taste my horse,
Who is to bear me like a thunderbolt
Against the bosom of the Prince of Wales.   125
Harry to Harry shall, hot horse to horse,
Meet, and ne'er part till one drop down a corse.
O that Glendower were come!

VERNON.   There is more news.
I learned in Worcester, as I rode along,   130
He cannot draw his power this fourteen days.°

DOUGLAS.   That's the worst tidings that I hear of yet.

WORCESTER.   Ay, by my faith, that bears a frosty° sound.

HOTSPUR.   What may the King's whole battle° reach unto?

VERNON.   To thirty thousand.   135

HOTSPUR.   Forty let it be.
My father and Glendower being both away,
The powers of us may serve so great a day.
Come, let us take a muster speedily.
Doomsday is near. Die all, die merrily.   140

DOUGLAS.   Talk not of dying. I am out of fear
Of death or death's hand for this one half year.   *Exeunt.*

Enter Falstaff [and] Bardolph.   IV ii

FALSTAFF.   Bardolph, get thee before° to Coventry; fill me a
bottle of sack. Our soldiers shall march through. We'll to
Sutton Co'fil' tonight.

BARDOLPH.   Will you give me money, captain?

FALSTAFF.   Lay out,° lay out.   5

---

120 mailèd Mars the war god in full
armor ("mail")
122 reprisal prize
131 draw . . . days muster his army for
another fourteen days

133 frosty chilling
134 battle army
IV ii 1 get thee before go on ahead
5 Lay out i.e. pay out of your pocket

BARDOLPH.   This bottle makes an angel.°

FALSTAFF.   And if it do, take it for thy labor; and if it make
twenty, take them all; I'll answer the coinage. Bid my lieu-
tenant Peto meet me at town's end.

BARDOLPH.   I will, captain. Farewell.   *Exit.* 10

FALSTAFF.   If I be not ashamed of my soldiers, I am a soused
gurnet.° I have misused the King's press° damnably. I have
got, in exchange of a hundred and fifty soldiers, three hundred and odd pounds. I press me none but good house-
holders, yeomen's sons;° inquire me out contracted 15
bachelors, such as had been asked twice on the banes°—
such a commodity of warm° slaves as had as lief hear the
devil as a drum, such as fear the report of a caliver° worse
than a struck fowl or a hurt wild duck. I pressed me none
but such toasts-and-butter,° with hearts in their bellies no 20
bigger than pins' heads, and they have bought out their
services; and now my whole charge consists of ancients,°
corporals, lieutenants, gentlemen of companies°—slaves as
ragged as Lazarus° in the painted cloth,° where the glut-
ton's dogs licked his sores; and such as indeed were never 25
soldiers, but discarded unjust° serving-men, younger sons
to younger brothers, revolted° tapsters, and ostlers trade-
fall'n;° the cankers° of a calm world and a long peace; ten
times more dishonorable ragged than an old fazed
ancient;° and such have I to fill up the rooms of them as 30
have bought out their services that you would think that I
had a hundred and fifty tattered prodigals lately come from
swine-keeping, from eating draff° and husks. A mad fellow
met me on the way, and told me I had unloaded all the

---

6 **angel** a coin worth, at various times,
six shillings eight pence to ten shillings
(Bardolph means that Falstaff now owes
him an angel, but Falstaff jokingly takes
"make" in the literal sense—as if the
bottle were minting angels; he tells Bardolph to take them all and he will guar-
antee they are not counterfeit)
11-12 **soused gurnet** pickled fish
12 **press** power of conscription
14-15 **good . . . sons** i.e. men of some
means who could pay to be let off
16 **asked . . . banes** i.e. on the verge of
marriage (banns [banes] were announce-
ments of intent to marry, published usually three times at weekly intervals)
17 **warm** comfortable

18 **caliver** musket
20 **toasts-and-butter** pampered mama's
boys
22 **ancients** ensigns, flag-bearers
23 **gentlemen of companies** lesser officers
24 **Lazarus** the beggar in the Dives par-
able (Luke 16:19-31)
24 **painted cloth** painted wall-hanging
26 **unjust** dishonest
27 **revolted** runaway
27-28 **trade-fall'n** unemployed
28 **cankers** parasites
29-30 **fazed ancient** tattered flag
33 **draff** pig-swill (the prodigal son, in
Luke 15:15-16, was so hungry he longed
for draff)

gibbets and pressed the dead bodies. No eye hath seen such 35
scarecrows. I'll not march through Coventry with them,
that's flat. Nay, and the villains march wide betwixt the
legs, as if they had gyves° on, for indeed I had the most of
them out of prison. There's not a shirt and a half in all
my company, and the half-shirt is two napkins tacked 40
together and thrown over the shoulders like a herald's coat
without sleeves; and the shirt, to say the truth, stol'n
from my host at Saint Albans, or the red-nose innkeeper of
Daventry. But that's all one; they'll find linen enough on
every hedge.°   45

Enter the Prince [and the] Lord of Westmoreland.

PRINCE.   How now, blown° Jack°? How now, quilt?

FALSTAFF.   What, Hal? How now, mad wag? What a devil dost
thou in Warwickshire? My good Lord of Westmoreland, I
cry you mercy.° I thought your honor had already been at
Shrewsbury.   50

WESTMORELAND.   Faith, Sir John, 'tis more than time that I
were there, and you too, but my powers are there already.
The King, I can tell you, looks for us all, we must away°
all night.

FALSTAFF.   Tut, never fear me: I am as vigilant as a cat to 55
steal cream.

PRINCE.   I think, to steal cream indeed, for thy theft hath
already made thee butter. But tell me, Jack, whose fellows
are these that come after?

FALSTAFF.   Mine, Hal, mine.   60

PRINCE.   I did never see such pitiful rascals.

FALSTAFF.   Tut, tut, good enough to toss;° food for powder,
food for powder, they'll fill a pit as well as better. Tush,
man, mortal men, mortal men.

WESTMORELAND.   Ay, but, Sir John, methinks they are exceed- 65
ing poor and bare,° too beggarly.

---

38 gyves fetters
45 hedge i.e. where linen was put out
to dry
46 blown (1) swelled (2) short of wind
46 Jack (1) Falstaff's name (2) soldier's
quilted jacket

48-49 I . . . mercy I beg your pardon
53 away be on our way
62 toss i.e. on the end of a pike
66 bare (1) threadbare (2) thin

FALSTAFF.   Faith, for their poverty, I know not where they had
that, and for their bareness, I am sure they never learned
that of me.

PRINCE.   No, I'll be sworn, unless you call three fingers° in the   70
ribs bare. But, sirrah, make haste. Percy is already in the
field.   *Exit.*

FALSTAFF.   What, is the King encamped?

WESTMORELAND.   He is, Sir John. I fear we shall stay too long.

FALSTAFF.   Well, to the latter end of a fray and the beginning   75
of a feast fits a dull° fighter and a keen guest.   *Exeunt.°*

Enter Hotspur, Worcester, Douglas, Vernon.   IV iii

HOTSPUR.   We'll fight with him tonight.

WORCESTER.   It may not be.°

DOUGLAS.   You give him then advantage.

VERNON.   Not a whit.°

HOTSPUR.   Why say you so? Looks he not for supply?°   5

VERNON.   So do we.

HOTSPUR.   His is certain, ours is doubtful.

WORCESTER.   Good cousin, be advised; stir not tonight.

VERNON.   Do not, my lord.

DOUGLAS.   You do not counsel well.   10
You speak it out of fear and cold heart.

VERNON.   Do me no slander, Douglas. By my life—
And I dare well maintain it with my life—
If well-respected° honor bid me on,
I hold as little counsel with weak fear   15
As you, my lord, or any Scot that this day lives.

---

70 **three fingers** i.e. of fat
76 **dull** uneager (opposed to "keen")
76 **s.d. Exeunt** (The quarto's "Exeunt,"
implying that Westmoreland goes off with
Falstaff, may be wrong; Falstaff's last
speech sounds as if Westmoreland has de-
parted and Falstaff winks at the audience)
IV iii 2 may not be can't be done
4 **Not a whit** not a bit
5 **supply** reinforcement
14 **well-respected** well-considered

Let it be seen tomorrow in the battle
Which of us fears.

DOUGLAS.   Yea, or tonight.

VERNON.   Content.°   20

HOTSPUR.   Tonight, say I.

VERNON.   Come, come, it may not be.
I wonder much, being men of such great leading° as you are,
That you foresee not what impediments
Drag back our expedition.° Certain horse°   25
Of my cousin Vernon's are not yet come up.
Your uncle Worcester's horse came but today;
And now their pride and mettle is asleep,
Their courage with hard labor tame and dull,
That not a horse is half the half of himself.   30

HOTSPUR.   So are the horses of the enemy
In general journey-bated° and brought low.
The better part of ours are full of rest.

WORCESTER.   The number of the King exceedeth ours.
For God's sake, cousin, stay till all come in.   35

                    The trumpet sounds a parley.

                Enter Sir Walter Blunt.

BLUNT.   I come with gracious offers from the King,
If you vouchsafe me hearing and respect.

HOTSPUR.   Welcome, Sir Walter Blunt, and would to God
You were of our determination.°
Some of us love you well; and even those some   40
Envy your great deservings and good name,
Because you are not of our quality,°
But stand against us like an enemy.

BLUNT.   And God defend° but still I should stand so,
So long as out of limit° and true rule   45
You stand against anointed majesty.
But to my charge.° The King hath sent to know

---

20 Content i.e. so be it, OK	**39 of our determination** on our side
23 leading leadership	**42 quality** company
25 expedition i.e. hastening into battle	**44 defend** forbid
25 horse cavalry	**45 limit** i.e. a subject's proper limits
32 journey-bated travel-weakened	**47 charge** message

The nature of your griefs,° and whereupon
You conjure° from the breast of civil peace
Such bold hostility, teaching his duteous land   50
Audacious cruelty.° If that the King
Have any way your good deserts° forgot,
Which he confesseth to be manifold,
He bids you name your griefs, and with all speed
You shall have your desires with interest,   55
And pardon absolute for yourself and these
Herein misled by your suggestion.°

HOTSPUR.   The King is kind, and well we know the King
Knows at which time to promise, when to pay.
My father and my uncle and myself   60
Did give him that same royalty he wears;
And when he was not six and twenty strong,
Sick in the world's regard, wretched and low,
A poor unminded° outlaw sneaking home,°
My father gave him welcome to the shore;   65
And when he heard him swear and vow to God
He came but to be Duke of Lancaster,
To sue his livery and beg his peace,°
With tears of innocency and terms of zeal,
My father, in kind heart and pity moved,   70
Swore him assistance, and performed it too.
Now when the lords and barons of the realm
Perceived Northumberland did lean to him,
The more and less° came in with cap and knee;°
Met him in boroughs, cities, villages,   75
Attended him on bridges, stood in lanes,°
Laid gifts before him, proffered him their oaths,°
Gave him their heirs as pages, followed him
Even at the heels in golden multitudes.
He presently, as greatness knows itself,°   80

---

48 **griefs** grievances
49 **conjure** call forth
51 **Audacious cruelty** a rash disposition
to be cruel
52 **deserts** deservings
57 **suggestion** instigation
64 **unminded** unnoted
64 **sneaking home** i.e. returning illegally
(from the exile abroad to which he had
been sent by Richard II)

68 **sue . . . peace** sue for the delivery
of his lands (which Richard II had ar-
rogated to the crown) and make his peace
with the king
74 **more and less** great and humble
74 **with . . . knee** i.e. with cap off and
bended knee (in token of allegiance)
76 **lanes** lines (on both sides of the road)
77 **oaths** pledges of loyalty
80 **as . . . itself** as greatness begins to
feel its strength

Steps me° a little higher than his vow
Made to my father, while his blood was poor,
Upon the naked shore at Ravenspurgh;
And now, forsooth, takes on him to reform
Some certain edicts and some strait° decrees   85
That lie too heavy on the commonwealth;
Cries out upon abuses, seems to weep
Over his country's wrongs; and by this face,°
This seeming brow of justice, did he win
The hearts of all that he did angle for;   90
Proceeded further—cut me° off the heads
Of all the favorites that the absent king
In deputation° left behind him here
When he was personal° in the Irish war.

BLUNT.   Tut! I came not to hear this.   95

HOTSPUR.   Then to the point.
In short time after, he deposed the King;
Soon after that deprived him of his life;
And in the neck of that° tasked° the whole state;
To make that worse, suff'red his kinsman March   100
(Who is, if every owner were well placed,
Indeed his king) to be engaged° in Wales,
There without ransom to lie forfeited;
Disgraced me in my happy victories,
Sought to entrap me by intelligence;°   105
Rated° mine uncle from the council board;
In rage dismissed my father from the court;
Broke oath on oath, committed wrong on wrong;
And in conclusion drove us to seek out
This head° of safety, and withal to pry   110
Into his title, the which we find
Too indirect° for long continuance.

BLUNT.   Shall I return this answer to the King?

---

81 **Steps me** steps
85 **strait** strict
88 **face** pretense
91 **cut me** cut
93 **In deputation** as deputies
94 **personal** personally engaged
99 **in . . . that** i.e. next
99 **tasked** taxed

102 **engaged** held hostage
105 **intelligence** spies (see I iii 34 ff)
106 **Rated** scolded (see I iii 15-21)
110 **head** army
112 **indirect** (1) not in the direct line
(from Richard) (2) morally oblique

HOTSPUR.   Not so, Sir Walter. We'll withdraw awhile.
　　Go to the King; and let there be impawned°   115
　　Some surety for a safe return again,
　　And in the morning early shall mine uncle
　　Bring him our purposes; and so farewell.

BLUNT.   I would you would accept of grace and love.

HOTSPUR.   And may be so we shall.   120

BLUNT.   Pray God you do.   [*Exeunt.*]

❧❧❧❧

　　　　Enter [the] Archbishop of York [and] Sir Michael.   *IV iv*

ARCHBISHOP.   Hie, good Sir Michael; bear this sealèd brief°
　　With wingèd haste to the Lord Marshal;
　　This to my cousin Scroop; and all the rest
　　To whom they are directed. If you knew
　　How much they do import, you would make haste.   5

SIR MICHAEL.   My good lord, I guess their tenor.°

ARCHBISHOP.   Like enough you do.
　　Tomorrow, good Sir Michael, is a day
　　Wherein the fortune of ten thousand men
　　Must bide the touch;° for, sir, at Shrewsbury,   10
　　As I am truly given to understand,
　　The King with mighty and quick-raisèd power
　　Meets with Lord Harry; and I fear, Sir Michael,
　　What with the sickness of Northumberland,
　　Whose power was in the first proportion,°   15
　　And what with Owen Glendower's absence thence,
　　Who with them was a rated sinew° too
　　And comes not in, overruled by prophecies—
　　I fear the power of Percy is too weak
　　To wage an instant° trial with the King.   20

---

115 **impawned** pledged
IV iv 1 brief message
6 tenor meaning
10 bide the touch stand the test (as
metal is tested by the touchstone to determine if it is gold)

15 proportion magnitude
17 rated sinew highly valued strength
20 instant immediate

SIR MICHAEL.   Why, my good lord, you need not fear;
   There is Douglas and Lord Mortimer.

ARCHBISHOP.   No, Mortimer is not there.

SIR MICHAEL.   But there is Mordake, Vernon, Lord Harry Percy,
   And there is my Lord of Worcester, and a head   25
   Of gallant warriors, noble gentlemen.

ARCHBISHOP.   And so there is; but yet the King hath drawn
   The special head° of all the land together—
   The Prince of Wales, Lord John of Lancaster,
   The noble Westmoreland and warlike Blunt,   30
   And many moe corrivals° and dear° men
   Of estimation and command in arms.

SIR MICHAEL.   Doubt not, my lord, they shall be well opposed.

ARCHBISHOP.   I hope no less, yet needful 'tis to fear;
   And, to prevent the worst, Sir Michael, speed.   35
   For if Lord Percy thrive not, ere the King
   Dismiss his power, he means to visit us,
   For he hath heard of our confederacy,°
   And 'tis but wisdom to make strong against him.
   Therefore make haste. I must go write again   40
   To other friends; and so farewell, Sir Michael.   *Exeunt.*

⁕~⁓~⁕~⁓~⁕

Enter the King, Prince of Wales, Lord John of Lancaster,   V i
   Earl of Westmoreland,° Sir Walter Blunt, Falstaff.

KING.   How bloodily° the sun begins to peer
   Above yon bulky hill! The day looks pale
   At his distemp'rature.°

PRINCE.   The southern wind
   Doth play the trumpet° to his° purposes   5

---

28 **head** army
31 **moe corrivals** more associates
31 **dear** important
38 **confederacy** i.e. in the rebellion
V i s.d. Earl of Westmoreland (In V ii 30
we learn that Westmoreland has been held
as the "surety" of IV iii 116, but at this
point Shakespeare apparently had not decided who was the hostage)
1 **bloodily** blood-red
3 **his distemp'rature** the sun's apparent
ailment
5 **play the trumpet** (1) act the announcer
(2) blow as if playing a trumpet
5 **his** the sun's

And by his hollow whistling in the leaves
Foretells a tempest and a blust'ring day.

KING.   Then with the losers let it sympathize,
For nothing can seem foul to those that win.

The trumpet sounds. Enter Worcester [and Vernon].

How now, my Lord of Worcester? 'Tis not well   10
That you and I should meet upon such terms
As now we meet. You have deceived our trust
And made us doff our easy robes of peace
To crush our old limbs in ungentle steel.
This is not well, my lord; this is not well.   15
What say you to it? Will you again unknit
This churlish knot of all-abhorrèd war,
And move in that obedient orb° again
Where you did give a fair and natural light,
And be no more an exhaled meteor,°   20
A prodigy of fear, and a portent
Of broachèd° mischief to the unborn times?°

WORCESTER.   Hear me, my liege.
For mine own part, I could be well content
To entertain the lag-end of my life   25
With quiet hours, for I protest
I have not sought the day of this dislike.°

KING.   You have not sought it! How comes it then?

FALSTAFF.   Rebellion lay in his way, and he found it.

PRINCE.   Peace, chewet,° peace!   30

WORCESTER.   It pleased your Majesty to turn your looks
Of favor from myself and all our house;
And yet I must remember° you, my lord,
We were the first and dearest of your friends.
For you my staff of office° did I break   35
In Richard's time, and posted day and night
To meet you on the way and kiss your hand
When yet you were in place and in account

---

18 **obedient orb** orbit of obedience
20 **exhaled meteor** wandering body (not subject to orbit, and thought an omen of "prodigy")
22 **broachèd** opened
22 **unborn times** future

27 **dislike** discord
30 **chewet** (1) jackdaw, i.e. chatterer (2) meat pie
33 **remember** remind
35 **staff of office** as steward to Richard II

Nothing so strong and fortunate as I.
It was myself, my brother, and his son   40
That brought you home and boldly did outdare°
The dangers of the time. You swore to us,
And you did swear that oath at Doncaster,
That you did nothing purpose 'gainst the state,
Nor claim no further than your new-fall'n° right,   45
The seat of Gaunt, dukedom of Lancaster.
To this we swore our aid. But in short space
It rained down fortune show'ring on your head,
And such a flood of greatness fell on you—
What with our help, what with the absent King,   50
What with the injuries° of a wanton time,
The seeming sufferances that you had borne,
And the contrarious winds that held the King
So long in his unlucky Irish wars
That all in England did repute° him dead—   55
And from this swarm of fair advantages
You took occasion to be quickly wooed
To gripe° the general sway into your hand;
Forgot your oath to us at Doncaster;
And, being fed by us, you used us so   60
As that ungentle gull,° the cuckoo's bird,°
Useth the sparrow—did oppress our nest,
Grew by our feeding to so great a bulk
That even our love durst not come near your sight
For fear of swallowing; but with nimble wing   65
We were enforced for safety sake to fly
Out of your sight and raise this present head;
Whereby we stand opposèd by such means
As you yourself have forged against yourself
By unkind usage, dangerous countenance,°   70
And violation of all faith and troth°
Sworn to us in your younger° enterprise.

---

41 outdare defy
45 new-fall'n i.e. by the death of his father, John of Gaunt
51 injuries evil doings
55 repute believe
58 gripe grab
61 gull, bird nestling (the cuckoo lays its eggs in other birds' nests, and the young cuckoos when hatched speedily destroy the other nestlings)
70 dangerous countenance hostile looks
71 troth pledges
72 younger earlier

KING.   These things, indeed, you have articulate,°
    Proclaimed at market crosses, read in churches,
    To face° the garment of rebellion   75
    With some fine color° that may please the eye
    Of fickle changelings° and poor discontents,
    Which gape and rub the elbow° at the news
    Of hurlyburly innovation.°
    And never did insurrection want   80
    Such water colors° to impaint his cause,
    Nor moody beggars, starving° for a time
    Of pell-mell havoc and confusion.

PRINCE.   In both your armies there is many a soul
    Shall pay full dearly for this encounter,   85
    If once they join in trial. Tell your nephew
    The Prince of Wales doth join with all the world
    In praise of Henry Percy. By my hopes,
    This present enterprise set off his head,°
    I do not think a braver gentleman,   90
    More active-valiant or more valiant-young,
    More daring or more bold, is now alive
    To grace this latter age° with noble deeds.
    For my part, I may speak it to my shame,
    I have a truant been to chivalry;   95
    And so I hear he doth account me too.
    Yet this before° my father's majesty—
    I am content that he shall take the odds
    Of his great name and estimation,°
    And will, to save the blood on either side,   100
    Try fortune with him in a single fight.

KING.   And, Prince of Wales, so dare we venture thee;°
    Albeit,° considerations infinite

---

73 **articulate** spelled out
75 **face** trim
76 **color** (1) hue (2) rhetorical coloring (hence, pretext)
77 **changelings** turncoats
78 **rub the elbow** i.e. hug themselves with delight
79 **innovation** revolution
81 **water colors** (1) pigments for "impainting" (2) thin or impermanent "show" (colors is used in the legal sense of a false but plausible plea in court, and in the sense of a calculated rhetoric full of ornamental figures of speech)
82 **starving** longing
89 **set . . . head** removed from his record
93 **this . . . age** these times
97 **this before** let me say this in the presence of
99 **estimation** reputation
102 **so . . . thee** so would we dare to back you
103 **Albeit** on the other hand

Do make against it. No, good Worcester, no!
We love our people well; even those we love   105
That are misled upon your cousin's part;
And, will they take the offer of our grace,°
Both he, and they, and you, yea, every man
Shall be my friend again, and I'll be his.
So tell your cousin, and bring me word   110
What he will do. But if he will not yield,
Rebuke and dread correction wait on us,°
And they shall do their office.° So be gone.
We will not now be troubled with reply.
We offer fair; take it advisedly.   115

                       Exit Worcester [with Vernon].

PRINCE.   It will not be accepted, on my life.
The Douglas and the Hotspur both together
Are confident against the world in arms.

KING.   Hence, therefore, every leader to his charge;
For, on their answer, will we set on them,   120
And God befriend us as our cause is just!

               Exeunt. Manent° Prince [and] Falstaff.

FALSTAFF.   Hal, if thou see me down in the battle and bestride
me,° so!° 'Tis a point of friendship.

PRINCE.   Nothing but a colossus can do thee that friendship.
Say thy prayers, and farewell.   115

FALSTAFF.   I would 'twere bedtime, Hal, and all well.

PRINCE.   Why, thou owest God a death.°   [*Exit.*]

FALSTAFF.   'Tis not due yet: I would be loath to pay him before
his day. What need I be so forward with him that calls
not on me? Well, 'tis no matter; honor pricks° me on. Yea,   130
but how if honor prick° me off when I come on? How
then? Can honor set to° a leg? No. Or an arm? No. Or
take away the grief° of a wound? No. Honor hath no skill
in surgery then? No. What is honor? A word. What is in

---

107   **grace** pardon
112   **wait on us** are in our service
113   **office** duty
121 s.d.   **Manent** remain
122-23   **bestride me** stand over me to fight off enemies
123   **so** i.e. I shan't object

127   **death** (pronounced like "debt," in which sense Falstaff takes it)
130   **pricks** spurs
131   **prick** check (as a casualty)
132   **set to** graft on, heal
133   **grief** pain

that word honor? What is that honor? Air—a trim° reckon- 135
ing! Who hath it? He that died a Wednesday. Doth he feel
it? No. Doth he hear it? No. 'Tis insensible then? Yea, to
the dead. But will it not live with the living? No. Why?
Detraction° will not suffer it. Therefore I'll none of it.
Honor is a mere scutcheon°—and so ends my catechism. 140
                                                                    Exit.

∽∼∾∼∾∼∾

Enter Worcester [and] Sir Richard Vernon.   **V** ii

WORCESTER.   O no, my nephew must not know, Sir Richard,
    The liberal and kind offer of the King.

VERNON.   'Twere best he did.

WORCESTER.   Then we are all undone.
    It is not possible, it cannot be,   5
    The King should keep his word in loving us.
    He will suspect us still° and find a time
    To punish this offense in other faults.°
    Supposition all our lives shall be stuck full of eyes;°
    For treason is but trusted like the fox,   10
    Who, never so tame, so cherished and locked up,
    Will have a wild trick° of his ancestors.
    Look how we can, or sad or° merrily,
    Interpretation will misquote our looks,
    And we shall feed like oxen at a stall,   15
    The better cherished still the nearer death.
    My nephew's trespass may be well forgot;
    It hath the excuse of youth and heat of blood,
    And an adopted name of privilege°—
    A hare-brained Hotspur, governed by a spleen.°   20
    All his offenses live upon my head

---

135 trim fine (spoken ironically)
139 Detraction slander
140 scutcheon painted shield with coat of
arms identifying a dead nobleman
V ii 7 still always
8 in . . . faults i.e. while pretending he
is punishing us for other offenses

9 Supposition . . . eyes suspicion will always be spying on us
12 trick (1) trait (2) wile
13 or sad or either sad or
19 an . . . privilege a nickname which
carries a privilege (to be impulsive) with it
20 spleen hot temper

And on his father's. We did train° him on;
And, his corruption being ta'en° from us,
We, as the spring of all, shall pay for all.
Therefore, good cousin, let not Harry know,   25
In any case, the offer of the King.

Enter Hotspur [and Douglas].

VERNON.   Deliver° what you will, I'll say 'tis so.
Here comes your cousin.

HOTSPUR.   My uncle is returned.
Deliver up my Lord of Westmoreland.°   30
Uncle, what news?

WORCESTER.   The King will bid you battle presently.

DOUGLAS.   Defy him by the Lord of Westmoreland.

HOTSPUR.   Lord Douglas, go you and tell him so.

DOUGLAS.   Marry, and shall, and very willingly.   *Exit.* 35

WORCESTER.   There is no seeming mercy in the King.

HOTSPUR.   Did you beg any? God forbid!

WORCESTER.   I told him gently of our grievances,
Of his oath-breaking, which he mended thus,
By now forswearing that he is forsworn.°   40
He calls us rebels, traitors, and will scourge
With haughty arms this hateful name in us.

Enter Douglas.

DOUGLAS.   Arm, gentlemen, to arms, for I have thrown
A brave defiance in King Henry's teeth,
And Westmoreland, that was engaged,° did bear it;   45
Which cannot choose but bring him quickly on.

WORCESTER.   The Prince of Wales stepped forth before the
    King
And, nephew, challenged you to single fight.

HOTSPUR.   O, would the quarrel lay upon our heads,
And that no man might draw short breath today   50

---

22 **train** (1) draw (2) aim
23 **ta'en** taken (like an infection)
27 **Deliver** report
30 **Westmoreland** (who has been hostage
for the safe return of Worcester and
Vernon)

40 **forswearing . . . forsworn** denying that
he went back on (his oath)
45 **engaged** held as a hostage

But I and Harry Monmouth! Tell me, tell me,
How showed his tasking?° Seemed it in contempt?

VERNON.   No, by my soul. I never in my life
Did hear a challenge urged more modestly,
Unless a brother should a brother dare   55
To gentle exercise and proof of arms.
He gave you all the duties of a man;°
Trimmed up your praises with a princely tongue;
Spoke your deservings like a chronicle;°
Making you ever better than his praise   60
By still dispraising praise valued with you;°
And, which became him like a prince indeed,
He made a blushing cital of° himself,
And chid his truant youth with such a grace
As if he mast'red there a double spirit   65
Of teaching and of learning instantly.°
There did he pause; but let me tell the world,
If he outlive the envy of this day,
England did never owe° so sweet a hope,
So much misconstrued in° his wantonness.   70

HOTSPUR.   Cousin, I think thou art enamorèd
On his follies. Never did I hear
Of any prince so wild a liberty.°
But be he as he will, yet once ere night
I will embrace him with a soldier's arm,   75
That° he shall shrink under my courtesy.
Arm, arm with speed! And, fellows, soldiers, friends,
Better consider what you have to do
Than I, that have not well the gift of tongue,
Can lift your blood up with persuasion.   80

                    Enter a Messenger.

MESSENGER.   My lord, here are letters for you.

HOTSPUR.   I cannot read them now.—
O gentlemen, the time of life is short!

---

52 **tasking** challenging
57 **duties . . . man** duties that one man
can owe another
59 **like a chronicle** i.e. with the itemized
characteristic of a chronicle history
61 **dispraising . . . you** i.e. because it
must fall so far short of your deservings

63 **cital of** reference to
66 **instantly** simultaneously
69 **owe** own
70 **in** with respect to
73 **liberty** reckless freedom
76 **That** so that

To spend that shortness basely were too long
If life did ride upon a dial's point,   85
Still ending at the arrival of an hour.°
And if we live, we live to tread on kings;
If die, brave° death, when princes die with us!
Now for our consciences, the arms are fair,
When the intent of bearing them is just.   90

     Enter another [Messenger].

MESSENGER. My lord, prepare. The King comes on apace.°

HOTSPUR. I thank him that he cuts me from my tale,
 For I profess not talking: only this—
 Let each man do his best; and here draw I
 A sword whose temper I intend to stain   95
 With the best blood that I can meet withal
 In the adventure° of this perilous day.
 Now, Esperance!° Percy! and set on.
 Sound all the lofty instruments of war,
 And by that music let us all embrace;   100
 For, heaven to earth,° some of us never shall
 A second time do such a courtesy.

   Here they embrace. The trumpets sound. [Exeunt.]

      ∽∼∾∾∼∽

   The King enters with his power. Alarum to the **V iii**
   battle. [Exeunt.] Then enter Douglas, and Sir
   Walter Blunt [disguised as the King].

BLUNT. What is thy name, that in battle thus thou crossest° me?
 What honor dost thou seek upon my head?

DOUGLAS. Know then my name is Douglas,
 And I do haunt thee in the battle thus
 Because some tell me that thou art a king.   5

84-86 **To . . . hour** if life were measured
by a clock's hand, closing after a single
hour, it would still be too long if basely
spent
88 **brave** glorious
91 **apace** fast

97 **adventure** risk
98 **Esperance** the Percy battle-cry (see II
iii 70)
101 **heaven to earth** the odds are as great
as heaven to earth
V iii 1 crossest single out

BLUNT.   They tell thee true.

DOUGLAS.   The Lord of Stafford dear today hath bought
   Thy likeness, for instead of thee, King Harry,
   This sword hath ended him: so shall it thee,
   Unless thou yield thee as my prisoner.   10

BLUNT.   I was not born a yielder, thou proud Scot;
   And thou shalt find° a king that will revenge
   Lord Stafford's death.

   They fight. Douglas kills Blunt. Then enter Hotspur.

HOTSPUR.   O Douglas, hadst thou fought at Holmedon thus,
   I never had triumphed upon a Scot.   15

DOUGLAS.   All's done, all's won: here breathless lies the King.

HOTSPUR.   Where?

DOUGLAS.   Here.

HOTSPUR.   This, Douglas? No. I know this face full well.
   A gallant knight he was, his name was Blunt;   20
   Semblably° furnished like the King himself.

DOUGLAS.   A fool° go with thy soul, whither it goes!
   A borrowed title hast thou bought too dear:
   Why didst thou tell me that thou wert a king?

HOTSPUR.   The King hath many marching in his coats.   25

DOUGLAS.   Now, by my sword, I will kill all his coats;
   I'll murder all his wardrobe, piece by piece,
   Until I meet the King.

HOTSPUR.   Up and away!
   Our soldiers stand full fairly for the day.   [*Exeunt.*] 30

   Alarum. Enter Falstaff solus.

FALSTAFF.   Though I could scape shot-free° at London, I fear
   the shot here. Here's no scoring° but upon the pate. Soft!
   Who are you? Sir Walter Blunt. There's honor for you!
   Here's no vanity!° I am as hot as molten lead, and as heavy
   too. God keep lead out of me. I need no more weight than   35
   mine own bowels. I have led my rag-of-muffins where they

---

12 **find** i.e. find in me
21 **Semblably** similarly
22 **fool** i.e. the title "fool" (spoken to Blunt's corpse)
31 **shot-free** (with pun on "shot" in the sense of tavern bill)

32 **scoring** (1) billing (2) striking
34 **Here's no vanity** (spoken ironically) i.e. here is "vanity"—futility, foolishness (but vanity also implies lightness, which is then set against the "heaviness" of life—see "lead," "heavy," "weight")

are peppered.° There's not three of my hundred and fifty
left alive, and they are for the town's end,° to beg during
life. But who comes here?

Enter the Prince.

PRINCE.   What, stands thou idle here? Lend me thy sword.   40
Many a nobleman lies stark and stiff
Under the hoofs of vaunting enemies, whose deaths are yet
unrevenged. I prithee lend me thy sword.

FALSTAFF.   O Hal, I prithee give me leave to breathe awhile.
Turk Gregory° never did such deeds in arms as I have done   45
this day. I have paid° Percy, I have made him sure.°

PRINCE.   He is indeed,° and living to kill thee.
I prithee lend me thy sword.

FALSTAFF.   Nay, before God, Hal, if Percy be alive, thou gets
not my sword; but take my pistol if thou wilt.   50

PRINCE.   Give it me. What, is it in the case?

FALSTAFF.   Ay, Hal. 'Tis hot, 'tis hot.° There's that will sack a
city.

The Prince draws it out and finds it to be a bottle of sack.

PRINCE.   What, is it a time to jest and dally now?
He throws the bottle at him. Exit.

FALSTAFF.   Well, if Percy be alive, I'll pierce° him. If he do   55
come in my way, so; if he do not, if I come in his willingly, let him make a carbonado° of me. I like not such
grinning honor as Sir Walter hath. Give me life; which if
I can save, so; if not, honor comes unlooked for, and
there's an end.   *[Exit.]*   60

36-37 I . . . peppered (a common practice of officers, who drew the dead soldiers' pay)
38 they . . . end being crippled, they'll
sit at the edge of town ("to beg during
life" from passersby)
45 Turk Gregory (In Shakespeare's time,
"Turk" was a byword for any ruthless man;
"Gregory" may refer to the irascible Pope
Gregory VII, or to Elizabeth's enemy, Pope
Gregory XIII; Pope and Turk were regarded
as the two great enemies of Protestant
Christendom)

46 paid killed
46 made him sure dispatched him
47 is indeed is indeed "sure," i.e. safe
52 hot i.e. he has fired it so often he
has had to put it away to cool
55 pierce (pronounced "perse")
57 carbonado meat slashed open for broil-
ing

Alarum. Excursions.° Enter the King, the Prince,   V *iv*
Lord John of Lancaster, Earl of Westmoreland.

KING.   I prithee, Harry, withdraw thyself, thou bleedest too
     much.
         Lord John of Lancaster, go you with him.

JOHN.   Not I, my lord, unless I did bleed too.

PRINCE.   I beseech your Majesty make up,°
     Lest your retirement° do amaze° your friends.   5

KING.   I will do so. My Lord of Westmoreland, lead him to his
     tent.

WESTMORELAND.   Come, my lord, I'll lead you to your tent.

PRINCE.   Lead me, my lord? I do not need your help;
     And God forbid a shallow scratch should drive   10
     The Prince of Wales from such a field as this,
     Where stained nobility lies trodden on,
     And rebels' arms triumph in massacres!

JOHN.   We breathe° too long. Come, cousin Westmoreland,
     Our duty this way lies. For God's sake, come.   15
                    [*Exeunt Lancaster and Westmoreland.*]

PRINCE.   By God, thou hast deceived me, Lancaster!
     I did not think thee lord of such a spirit.
     Before, I loved thee as a brother, John,
     But now I do respect thee as my soul.

KING.   I saw him hold Lord Percy at the point   20
     With lustier maintenance° than I did look for
     Of such an ungrown warrior.

PRINCE.   O, this boy lends mettle to us all!   *Exit.*
                    [*Enter Douglas.*]

DOUGLAS.   Another king? They grow like Hydra's° heads.
     I am the Douglas, fatal to all those   25

V iv s.d. **Excursions** sorties   14 **breathe** pause
4 **make up** move forward   21 **maintenance** bearing
5 **retirement** withdrawal   24 **Hydra** a many-headed monster which
5 **amaze** dismay   grew two heads for each one destroyed

That wear those colors on them. What art thou
That counterfeit'st the person of a king?

KING.   The King himself, who, Douglas, grieves at heart
   So many of his shadows thou hast met,
   And not the very King. I have two boys   30
   Seek Percy and thyself about the field;
   But, seeing thou fall'st on me so luckily,
   I will assay° thee, and defend thyself.

DOUGLAS.   I fear thou art another counterfeit;
   And yet, in faith, thou bearest thee like a king. 35
   But mine I am sure thou art, whoe'er thou be,
   And thus I win thee.

They fight, the King being in danger. Enter Prince of Wales.

PRINCE.   Hold up thy head, vile Scot, or thou art like
   Never to hold it up again. The spirits
   Of valiant Shirley, Stafford, Blunt° are in my arms. 40
   It is the Prince of Wales that threatens thee,
   Who never promiseth but he means to pay.
          They fight: Douglas flieth.
   Cheerly,° my lord. How fares your Grace?
   Sir Nicholas Gawsey hath for succor sent,
   And so hath Clifton. I'll to Clifton straight.   45

KING.   Stay and breathe awhile.
   Thou hast redeemed thy lost opinion,°
   And showed thou mak'st some tender° of my life,
   In this fair rescue thou hast brought to me.

PRINCE.   O God, they did me too much injury   50
   That ever said I heark'ned for° your death.
   If it were so, I might have let alone
   The insulting hand of Douglas over you,
   Which would have been as speedy in your end
   As all the poisonous potions in the world,   55
   And saved the treacherous labor of your son.

KING.   Make up to Clifton; I'll to Sir Nicholas Gawsey. *Exit.*

Enter Hotspur.

---

33 **assay** try
40 **Shirley, Stafford, Blunt** (those whom Douglas has killed wearing the King's coats)
43 **Cheerly** look cheerily
47 **opinion** reputation
48 **tender** value
51 **heark'ned for** listened for, wished

HOTSPUR.   If I mistake not, thou art Harry Monmouth.

PRINCE.   Thou speak'st as if I would deny my name.

HOTSPUR.   My name is Harry Percy.   60

PRINCE.   Why, then I see a very valiant rebel of the name.
      I am the Prince of Wales, and think not, Percy,
      To share with me in glory any more.
      Two stars keep not their motion in one sphere,°
      Nor can one England brook° a double reign   65
      Of Harry Percy and the Prince of Wales.

HOTSPUR.   Nor shall it, Harry, for the hour is come
      To end the one of us; and would to God
      Thy name in arms were now as great as mine!

PRINCE.   I'll make it greater ere I part from thee,   70
      And all the budding honors on thy crest
      I'll crop to make a garland for my head.

HOTSPUR.   I can no longer brook thy vanities.°   *They fight.*

Enter Falstaff.

FALSTAFF.   Well said,° Hal! To it, Hal! Nay, you shall find no
      boy's play here, I can tell you.   75

*Enter Douglas. He fighteth with Falstaff [who]
falls down as if he were dead. [Exit Douglas.]
The Prince killeth Percy.*

HOTSPUR.   O Harry, thou hast robbed me of my youth!
      I better brook the loss of brittle life
      Than those proud titles thou hast won of me.
      They wound my thoughts worse than thy sword my flesh.
      But thoughts, the slaves of life, and life, time's fool,°   80
      And time, that takes survey of all the world,
      Must have a stop. O, I could prophesy,
      But that the earthy and cold hand of death
      Lies on my tongue. No, Percy, thou art dust,
      And food for—   *[Dies.]* 85

PRINCE.   For worms, brave Percy. Fare thee well, great heart.
      Ill-weaved ambition, how much art thou shrunk!
      When that this body did contain a spirit,

---

64   **sphere**   orbit
65   **brook**   put up with
73   **vanities**   boasts
74   **said**   done

80   **slaves . . . fool**   i.e. because thoughts
are dependent on life and because life is
subservient to time

A kingdom for it was too small a bound;
But now two paces of the vilest earth   90
Is room enough. This earth that bears thee dead
Bears not alive so stout° a gentleman.
If thou wert sensible° of courtesy,
I should not make so dear° a show of zeal.
But let my favors° hide thy mangled face;   95
And, even in thy behalf, I'll thank myself
For doing these fair rites of tenderness.
Adieu, and take thy praise with thee to heaven.
Thy ignominy sleep with thee in the grave,
But not rememb'red in thy epitaph.   100

                    He spieth Falstaff on the ground.

What, old acquaintance? Could not all this flesh
Keep in a little life? Poor Jack, farewell!
I could have better spared a better man.
O, I should have a heavy miss° of thee
If I were much in love with vanity.°   105
Death hath not struck so fat a deer° today,
Though many dearer,° in this bloody fray.
Emboweled° will I see thee by-and-by;
Till then in blood by noble Percy lie.   *Exit.*

                    Falstaff riseth up.

FALSTAFF. Emboweled? If thou embowel me today, I'll give you 110
leave to powder° me and eat me too tomorrow. 'Sblood,
'twas time to counterfeit,° or that hot termagant° Scot had
paid me scot and lot° too. Counterfeit? I lie; I am no
counterfeit. To die is to be a counterfeit, for he is but the
counterfeit of a man who hath not the life of a man; but 115
to counterfeit dying when a man thereby liveth, is to be
no counterfeit, but the true and perfect image of life
indeed. The better part of valor is discretion,° in the which

---

92 **stout** valiant
93 **sensible** aware
94 **dear** heartfelt
95 **favors** (probably Hal's ostrich plumes, his emblem as Prince of Wales)
104 **heavy miss** "heavy" loss (in two senses)
105 **vanity** frivolity (and lightness)
106 **deer** (with pun on "dear")
107 **dearer** nobler, more valuable
108 **Emboweled** disemboweled (for embalming)

111 **powder** salt
112 **counterfeit** pretend
112 **termagant** bloodthirsty
113 **paid . . . lot** killed me (literally, paid me in full; "scot" and "lot" were parish taxes)
118 **The . . . discretion** (Falstaff willfully misinterprets the maxim that valor is better for being accompanied by discretion)

better part I have saved my life. Zounds, I am afraid of
this gunpowder Percy, though he be dead. How if he should 120
counterfeit too, and rise? By my faith, I am afraid he
would prove the better counterfeit. Therefore I'll make him
sure; yea, and I'll swear I killed him. Why may not he
rise as well as I? Nothing confutes° me but eyes, and
nobody sees me. Therefore, sirrah [*stabs him*], with a new 125
wound in your thigh, come you along with me.

> *He takes up Hotspur on his back. Enter*
> *Prince [and] John of Lancaster.*

PRINCE.   Come, brother John; full bravely has thou fleshed
Thy maiden sword.

JOHN.   But, soft! whom have we here?
Did you not tell me this fat man was dead?   130

PRINCE.   I did, I saw him dead,
Breathless and bleeding on the ground. Art thou alive,
Or is it fantasy that plays upon our eyesight?
I prithee speak. We will not trust our eyes
Without our ears. Thou art not what thou seem'st.   135

FALSTAFF.   No, that's certain, I am not a double man;° but if I
be not Jack Falstaff, then am I a Jack.° There is Percy. If
your father will do me any honor, so; if not, let him kill
the next Percy himself. I look to be either earl or duke, I
can assure you.   140

PRINCE.   Why, Percy I killed myself, and saw thee dead!

FALSTAFF.   Didst thou? Lord, Lord, how this world is given to
lying. I grant you I was down, and out of breath, and so
was he; but we rose both at an instant and fought a long
hour by Shrewsbury clock. If I may be believed, so; if not, 145
let them that should reward valor bear the sin upon their
own heads. I'll take it upon my death, I gave him this
wound in the thigh. If the man were alive and would deny
it, zounds; I would make him eat a piece of my sword.

JOHN.   This is the strangest tale that ever I heard.   150

---

124 **confutes** can contradict
136 **double man** (1) wraith (2) twofold
man
137 **Jack** rascal

PRINCE.   This is the strangest fellow, brother John.
          Come, bring your luggage nobly on your back.
          For my part, if a lie may do thee grace,°
          I'll gild it with the happiest terms I have.
                                          A retreat is sounded.
          The trumpet sounds retreat; the day is ours.   155
          Come, brother, let us to the highest of the field,
          To see what friends are living, who are dead.
                              Exeunt [Prince Henry and Prince John].

FALSTAFF.   I'll follow,° as they say, for reward. He that rewards
          me, God reward him. If I do grow great, I'll grow less; for
          I'll purge,° and leave sack, and live cleanly, as a nobleman 160
          should do.   *Exit [bearing off the body].*

                        ❦❦❦❦❦

          The trumpets sound. Enter the King, Prince of   V v
          Wales, Lord John of Lancaster, Earl of West-
          moreland, with Worcester and Vernon prisoners.

KING.   Thus ever did rebellion find rebuke.
        Ill-spirited Worcester, did not we send grace,
        Pardon, and terms of love to all of you?
        And wouldst thou turn our offers contrary?
        Misuse the tenor° of thy kinsman's trust?   5
        Three knights upon our party slain today,
        A noble earl, and many a creature else
        Had been alive this hour,
        If like a Christian thou hadst truly borne
        Betwixt our armies true intelligence.°   10

WORCESTER.   What I have done my safety urged me to;
        And I embrace this fortune patiently,
        Since not to be avoided it falls on me.

---

153 **grace** credit   **V v 5 tenor** intended purpose
158 **follow** i.e. as hounds do when the   **10 intelligence** information
quarry is killed, to receive their reward
160 **purge** repent

KING.   Bear Worcester to the death, and Vernon too;
    Other offenders we will pause upon.   15
                  [Exeunt Worcester and Vernon, guarded].
    How goes the field?

PRINCE.   The noble Scot, Lord Douglas, when he saw
    The fortune of the day quite turned from him,
    The noble Percy slain, and all his men
    Upon the foot of fear, fled with the rest;   20
    And falling from a hill, he was so bruised
    That the pursuers took him. At my tent
    The Douglas is, and I beseech your Grace
    I may dispose of him.

KING.   With all my heart.   25

PRINCE.   Then, brother John of Lancaster, to you
    This honorable bounty° shall belong.
    Go to the Douglas and deliver him
    Up to his pleasure,° ransomless and free.
    His valors shown upon our crests today   30
    Have taught us how to cherish such high deeds,
    Even in the bosom of our adversaries.

JOHN.   I thank your Grace for this high courtesy,
    Which I shall give away immediately.

KING.   Then this remains, that we divide our power.   35
    You, son John, and my cousin Westmoreland,
    Towards York shall bend you with your dearest speed
    To meet Northumberland and the prelate Scroop,
    Who, as we hear, are busily in arms.
    Myself and you, son Harry, will towards Wales   40
    To fight with Glendower and the Earl of March.
    Rebellion in this land shall lose his sway,
    Meeting the check of such another day;
    And since this business° so fair is done,
    Let us not leave till all our own be won.   *Exeunt.*   45

---

27 **bounty** kind act
28-29 **deliver . . . pleasure** let him be his
own master
44 **business** (trisyllabic)

IN THE THEATER OF THE MIND

The comments that follow are meant to suggest ways of internally *visualizing* and *feeling* the play, which are essential if the reading of it is not to be merely an intellectual exercise. Few of us get a chance to see professional productions of Shakespeare, and that's a pity; the lines well spoken, the parts well acted have a profound impact that is hard to duplicate in the study. Nevertheless, the life of a Shakespearean play *is* in the lines, and an imaginative reader can realize that life in the theater of his own mind. Shakespeare's Globe demanded of the audience a ready ear and an inward eye—a willingness to transcend what they saw before them in order to transform it imaginatively into a world that neither eye nor ear actually quite caught. A reader can do the same, and, once he has learned how, is better off in doing it for himself by the activity of his own imagination than he is in passively allowing a stage or film director to do it for him. Even the greatest of professional productions remains subject, in the end, to the image of the play's potentialities that exists in a seasoned playgoer's, or a seasoned reader's, mind.

Since we are not directly concerned here with how the play should be produced in the theater, but rather how parts of it may be realized in the imagination, we refer to actual staging only to point out what the language indicates is going on inside and outside the characters. On the same grounds, we make no attempt to "cover" the total action in any chronological way. Our observations on particular scenes are intended to suggest ways of looking at others as well.

ii

Shakespeare's aim in *1 Henry IV* is to dramatize the fact that no lasting order in the political or moral realm can be built on disorder, and for this purpose his multiple and shifting plot line affords him a perfect visual representation. As the worlds of Henry's court, Hotspur's rebellious crew, and Falstaff's tavern cronies succeed one another, we quickly come to realize that each is being more and more fully revealed to us from a variety of angles and more and more definitively evaluated. We also realize, though much more gradually, that Prince Hal is the figure against whom in the long run all the rest are to be measured—not because he is perfect and they are imperfect (he has his father's political streak, we notice), but because he shows himself capable of absorbing the best from all three of the worlds in which he is involved: court, camp, and tavern. In short, he is a person who grows, whereas, in all circumstances, his father, Hotspur, and Falstaff continue to be pretty much what they always were. The plot line of the play, then, is designed to give us three environments, each with its special virtues and vices, among which Hal can move, until gradually they all merge on the battlefield and in him.

iii

The specific ways in which the juxtaposition of scenes works in this play may be seen at a glance from Act I, where the first scene has no sooner made its impression on us than it is qualified and commented upon by scenes ii and iii. The opening lines of the first scene foresee a time of peace:

> So shaken as we are, so wan with care,
> Find we a time for frighted peace to pant
> And breathe short-winded accents of new broils
> To be commenced in stronds afar remote.

But there is no peace, nor is there likely to be any so long as the disorders set abroad by Henry's usurpation of the throne and his murder of his predecessor (Richard II) continue to poison the land with lawlessness and bloodshed—all caught for us unforgettably in his first lines, which deny peace even as they pay it lip-service: English soil is daubed "with her own chil-

dren's blood"; "trenching war" has channeled her fields and
enveloped her people in "the furious close of civil butchery"; a
thousand men in Wales lie "butcherèd," their corpses dishonored
by "beastly shameless transformation"; "ten thousand bold
Scots" are already "balked in their own blood." If we have our
ears open not only to what the reports tell us but also to their
language, we know that peace will always be "frighted" in the
company of such men as these. Even Henry's expiatory crusade
to the Holy Land will be only another "broil," though carried
on at a distance.

We notice that while the stage is peopled from the beginning with a full royal retinue, only Henry and Westmoreland
speak. We are evidently in the London palace, and the throne
might well be featured for our benefit in the center of the stage
—with Henry moving restlessly in front of it. As he turns to
one matter of business after another, he conveys to us a sense
of strong leadership, and then, as the reports of disorder and
disobedience (not only of the Scots and Welsh, but his own
son) multiply, a sense of strong leadership up against unruly
forces that are responses to—even in a way reflections of—his
own unruly self-will in revolting against Richard. It will, therefore, be symbolically important if we never see him actually
occupying the stolen throne, but always in one way or other
striving to defend it. The order he has foretold in his opening
speech is thus soon seen as empty talk, ironically foretelling
the future as a continuation of the past and not a respite from it.

Scene i is Henry's scene, Westmoreland serving mainly
as his sometime dummy. His dominating presence and his view
of king-subject relations must monopolize the mind's stage, and
the whole scene must serve to hint at the corrupting of lawlessness to beget lawlessness.

iv

We can assume that scene i takes place in the King's
palace in London, but there is no indication in the text as to
where scene ii takes place, nor does it matter. The fact that
place is of no significance seems to be part of the dramatic
point, for in all three of these scenes what is played is a variation on a single theme with changing principals; and the fluid,
unlocalized Elizabethan stage would have encouraged our aware-

ness of this "similarity-with-a-difference." The throne might well remain on stage, in the shadows, as it were, a visual suggestion that "the most comparative, rascalliest, sweet young prince" we see here will one day occupy it, although his personal qualifications remain shadowy and suspect because of what his father has just said about him and what we now see him involved in.

If the language of scene i tells us that the King's world is bloody, violent, full of duplicity and greed, the language of scene ii suggests a related kind of disorder; worse in the eyes of the King or Hotspur, but in many ways really superior. Wit and a vulgar sagacity strike from every line. The language flows with exuberance and sensuality, with an aggressive amorality that breathes a fresher spirit than all the high-sounding assertiveness of either the self-righteous King or the choleric Hotspur. And yet we are constantly aware that it is wit in the service of self-indulgence and one-upmanship. Falstaff and the Prince are playing games, and the trick for us as audience is to delight in the Falstaff who can out-fence the Prince verbally, while not being so seduced by the man's charm that we forget what he is and does; and also to acknowledge the depth of Hal's delight in Falstaff and his world, while recognizing that he is in no sense blatantly amoral like Falstaff and keeps the "huge bombard of sack" at arm's length all the time.

Falstaff's very size makes physical closeness impossible. He is mountainously fat—on the one hand awesomely attractive, on the other repellent, as most greatly oversized people are. In contrast, Hal is lean and hard, with obvious grace and dignity even as he trades in tavern wit. The problem in I ii is to keep uppermost the distinction between the Crown Prince and the clown prince. Though the throne remains in the shadows, it might be well to have Hal's movements seen as always keeping himself between that shadow and Falstaff, suggesting visually, even before his soliloquy at the close of the scene, that he will keep its majesty unsullied by base behavior. After the departure of Poins, the throne might be seen more clearly as if it were an exteriorized image of what is in his mind during the soliloquy.

The distance between Hal and Falstaff grows greater as the play progresses, and the distancing is handled verbally by a steady shift in the language Hal uses toward him. Here in I ii he takes an obvious delight in matching wit for wit. In the robbery scene (II ii) and the long tavern scene (II iv) there's more sharpness and more matter in the barbs. After II iv the two men are together only briefly, and by Act V the Prince no longer bandies with him, although he continues to treat him kindly. Falstaff does not leave the play, but the Prince leaves Falstaff, as he says in I ii he will do when the time calls for it (180-202). All through their scenes together the question of Hal's relationship to Falstaff must be imaginatively kept in mind: both what they have in common (wit, warmth, exuberance, independence, self-understanding, self-sufficiency, disdain of self-puffery) and where they differ (irresponsibility, self-indulgence, mock-honor, grossness).

I iii returns us immediately to another royal audience, this time with the summoned rebel lords. Again the throne is in full view, with Henry again not seated on it, but perhaps centered in front of it, and again he speaks first—bluntly, commandingly, self-righteously. The King's words are about disorder and disobedience, and they are both right and ironic, as are Hotspur's in defense of his behavior toward the prisoners. This breed of rebels is a direct threat to Henry's kingship, not the shadowy, symbolic threat that the tavern world is. We might see this difference not only in the fact that the throne is physically there, in the center of the action, but also in possible movements that Hotspur makes toward it as he explains himself. The throne is empty; he can easily, and with no conscious intention of staking an emblematic claim, put his hand on it as he finishes his scornful commentary on the "certain lord" with the unconscious irony of:

> . . . let not his report
> Come current for an accusation
> Betwixt my love and your high Majesty. (I iii 68-70)

Henry's dismissal of Hotspur's explanation and his scathing comments on Mortimer, Hotspur's brother-in-law, can follow as he himself moves unconsciously toward the throne and lays his hand on the opposite side, confronting the young rebel across the prize that both wish to control. As in scene i, Henry remains aggressively conscious of the fact that he is King (his curt dismissal of Worcester at the very beginning of the scene attests to that), but in the confrontation with Hotspur, especially with the area of the throne now co-occupied by this unawed and undeferential young man (Worcester had been dismissed for only the slightest kind of protesting comment), we get a strong visual suggestion that Henry is not as securely in command as his words suggest. If again, as in scene i, the remainder of Henry's retinue keep motionless, holding themselves apart from the center of attention (with Blunt's conciliatory comment coming from behind Henry so that the King's not even turning toward the speaker can suggest that he pays little attention to the comment), then the visual intrusion of Hotspur into the throne area—the power area—will carry the full irony that it is just this young man, whom Henry has praised in contrasting him with his own Harry in scene i, who now most sharply challenges the King—and right in his own court.

Henry's response to Hotspur's defense of Mortimer is a curt tongue-lashing. He accuses Hotspur of boldface lying, and lays down commands as if dealing with a defiant child. We see Hotspur's hand tightening on the throne arm as Henry berates him and finally dealing that same arm a resounding smack as he explodes with "And if the devil come and roar for them,/I will not send them" (125-26) after Henry sweeps from the room with his blunt threats ringing in the rebels' ears.

The fact that Henry vacates the throne room and that the rest of the scene takes place there should not be lost on us. As Hotspur fulminates and as his father and uncle calmly reveal the preparations for rebellion that make a mockery of their pratings of hurt pride at Henry's suspicion and overbearing attitude, we see that the quality of the men who contest for this throne is poor indeed, and that at this point there is no one in sight who genuinely deserves to occupy it. After they leave, a brief moment with the throne spotlighted drives home hard what the first act has with multiple effect implied—that for all the King's mastery the kingdom is masterless.

One final effect of Act I should also not be lost on us. Hal is physically absent when one might well expect him to be present—e.g. at court when major affairs of the kingdom are being deliberated. Though out of sight, he is by no means out of mind; though Henry deplores his behavior openly and at length in scene i, and Hotspur speaks disparagingly of him in scene iii, we know better than both, having heard his soliloquy in scene ii. Our awareness of what he tells us he is determined to become gives a special meaning to his physical absence in scenes where he is symbolically present.

v

Act II drives home in noisy detail the decay and disorder whose root causes have been shown us in I. The inn at Rochester (II i) "is turned upside down since Robin Ostler died": there's no proper service, no friendly help among travelers—just shouts and insults and open-eyed recognition that it's every man for himself. The robbery scene (II ii) is even more topsy-turvy. "Brawling" at the top of his lungs, cursing the fact that he has nowhere to seat his "fat guts," Falstaff fixes the tone of the whole act in his frustrated bellowing: "A plague upon it when thieves cannot be true one to another!" (24-25) The scene with Hotspur and his wife (II iii) that immediately follows should keep something of the same key. Hotspur is as unbridled and blustering as the tavern crowd, and his reaction to the weaseling in the letter from the "frosty-spirited rogue" echoes Falstaff's reaction to his treatment by Poins and Hal. As Falstaff's alter ego, Hotspur shows another side of disorder and riot.

All these scenes are high-spirited and funny, but it would be a mistake *not* to see that the humor is at the service of incisive comment on Henry's kingdom and on the significance of the unmanned throne. Just as Hal was physically missing, yet clearly in the mind's eye, in I i and iii, so Henry, though missing in II i-iii, is clearly in the imaginative background: it is *his* "commonwealth" that the brigands "ride up and down on," *his* "exchequer" that is being bilked, and *his* kingdom that Hotspur is threatening to dismantle. In each instance, the lack of awe or respect for what the King is and should be, whether in flippant or defiant terms, throws light on the lawlessness rampant in the realm.

All three scenes lead to the central scene of the play, II iv, where all the attitudes we have been talking about thrive, but where there are also sure signs that some semblance of order will ultimately prevail. The same high spirit marks the language of the scene, but it is progressively tempered by unmistakable sobering notes, not the least of which is that the humor lacks the harshness it has been tinged with in scenes i-iii. With the "play extempore," the comic vein of Act II meets with the political vein that dominated Act I, and once again we have the throne as the center of our attention. Falstaff and Hal take turns playing King and Prince, and we get the first of many "counter-

feit" Henrys who will come again on the battlefield in Act V.
We see Falstaff determine what the throne will be ("This chair
shall be my state, this dagger my scepter, and this cushion my
crown" [353-54]); but Hal determines what the ludicrous sight
means, and whether he speaks his lines to the general company
or as an aside, the effect is the same: "Thy state is taken for a
joined-stool, thy golden scepter for a leaden dagger, and thy
precious rich crown for a pitiful bald crown" (355-57). Falstaff
should be seated on his mock throne when these words are
spoken, and we should be immediately aware of what his presence there tells us: he is a counterfeit king, as Henry the
usurper is; he has, however, a kind of warmth, wit, and lack of
pomposity that are appropriate to the position; unhappily, like a
child, he can think only of himself. His characterization of the
"goodly portly man" reminds us of both his ingratiating sense of
humor about himself and his inability to think beyond himself,
as does his later poignant self-defense:

> ... No, my good lord: banish Peto, banish Bardolph,
> banish Poins; but for sweet Jack Falstaff, kind Jack
> Falstaff, true Jack Falstaff, valiant Jack Falstaff,
> and therefore more valiant being, as he is, old Jack
> Falstaff, banish not him thy Harry's company . . .
> banish plump Jack, and banish all the world!
> (443-49)

When Hal assumes the makeshift throne, the leaden dagger and cushion crown are discarded, and misrule is symbolically banished with the simple assertion, "Well, here I am set."
We can see the company visibly stiffen (there's no chirping
here from the Hostess—"O Jesu, this is excellent sport"). Falstaff's answering line, "And here I stand. Judge, my masters" is
almost ominous, and he gets more than he asked for. Hal's
words as counterfeit king to unruly prince are prophetically—
intentionally?—the words of the future king to an unruly subject: "Swearest thou, ungracious boy? Henceforth ne'er look at
me. Thou art violently carried away from grace. . . ." The political world has taken over, and Hal's brief, "I do, I will" in answer
to Falstaff's "banish not him thy Harry's company" marks its
ascendancy. If Hal stays seated on the tavern throne when the
sheriff enters, we are reminded visually that order will be
restored (so, on a more mundane level, will the stolen money)
"with advantage."

We pass immediately to another kind of king-playing in III i with the play's second round of rebellion brewing, this time with Glendower and Mortimer (whom Richard had proclaimed "heir to the throne") as participants. Again, as in II ii, it is Henry's kingdom that is being dismantled, and the scene opens with immediate reference to the map that this triumvirate will mark up into shares. The irony that a dismembered kingdom is *no* kingdom is sharpened for us as we see the three men huddled over the paper, quibbling like school boys over who is to get the biggest piece.

There's a sobering poignancy to the humor at the end of II iv that is totally lacking in III i. We laugh openly at the tavern hijinks because we know that Hal's enthusiasm for low-life vitality is qualified by his recognition that such behavior has no place near a throne. Our laughter at the rebels' bickering is muted by our recognition that these great egos take themselves quite seriously, as we must also, despite the dramatic demonstration that much of their behavior is shamefully childish.

What we see in II iv put against what we see in III i tells us that the Prince is more than a match for these self-deceived plotters. III ii confirms that impression unmistakably, and adds the further one that Hal has his father's strong sense of himself as able to take command, without his father's blindness to his own nature and his simplicity about why men do what they do. In III ii we return to the court and the visual reminder that the throne in stage center is the focal point of the play. In Henry's cataloguing of what he has done and what his son has and has not done, we get an echo of the self-satisfaction we heard throughout III i, but Hal's rejoinder (130-60) strikes another note entirely. He takes his father's baseless charge (122-29) and shows how meanly conceived the calculated taunt was by answering it in blunt, positive, and yet respectful terms that stress a concern for what, as Prince, he must *be* rather than for what he must do to build a reputation. That the King has the grace and sense to recognize the import of the words ("A hundred thousand rebels die in this!/Thou shalt have charge and sovereign trust herein" [161-62]) shows how genuine they are. If, during the rejoinder, Hal moves clearly into the throne area (occupied before by the King only), we are reminded visually that what he foretells will come true. This is the last we see of the court or the throne. Symbolically, both move with the King and Hal to Shrewsbury, where, quite literally, the throne is up for grabs, and Hal becomes, as the savior of his father, its chief defender.

vi

If the leading business of the play is the maturing of the Prince in preparation for creative kingship, then its last three scenes show how fully he has mastered its three worlds of court, field, and tavern. We know how far he has come and where he will go as we see him in action on the Shrewsbury battlefield, a commanding presence who makes no claims to being such, unlike his father earlier in the play. In V iii, the counterfeiting machinations of the King are set alongside the moving but vainglorious heroics of Douglas and Blunt, the unfounded assurance of Hotspur that "Our soldiers stand full fairly for the day" (30), and the anti-heroic hide-saving of Falstaff. In contrast, the brief appearance of the Prince, with his instinctive feel for the dangers and needs of the situation and his clear understanding that mockery and buffoonery are out of place ("What, is it a time to jest and dally now?" [54]), shows how different he is from all the rest.

In scene iv he physically dominates the action, and this must be brought out visually, perhaps by means of the helmet whose ostrich plumes (emblem of the heir to the throne then, as now) are mentioned several times and finally used to hide the "mangled face" of Hotspur. He is all energy and decision: his wounds mean nothing ("a shallow scratch"); he fights so fiercely that even Douglas flees; he saves his father's life, praises his brother's valor, keeps track of allies in need. The crowning of the scene is the triumphant Prince astride the fallen Hotspur, gazing at the counterfeit Falstaff, magnanimous to both, but keenly alive to their grievous personal failings. Scene v completes the picture of the grown-up Prince in a still imperfect, war-filled world: courtly, valorous, strong-minded, and great of heart.

STUDY QUESTIONS

ESSAY QUESTIONS

1. Take as your lead any of the following comments on *1 Henry IV* and write a paper developing the idea, or qualifying it, or refuting it—or a combination of all three.

   (a) "Falstaff was no coward, but pretended to be one merely for the sake of trying experiments on the credulity of mankind: he was a liar with the same object, and not because he loved falsehood for itself. He was a man of such preeminent abilities, as to give him a profound contempt for all those by whom he was usually surrounded, and to lead to a determination on his part, in spite of their fancied superiority, to make them his tools and dupes."

   (b) ". . . the equivocal Falstaff is the essential Falstaff. He is never twice quite the same; he is a series of impersonations. He is an inveterate comic actor and every man is a stooge who must play up to him."

   (c) ". . . no man is more dangerous than he that, with a will to corrupt, hath the power to please; and . . . neither wit nor honesty ought to think themselves safe with such a companion when they see Henry seduced by Falstaff."

   (d) "The advantage to the actor who plays Hotspur, and the disadvantage to the actor who plays the prince, is enormous. Hotspur is by far the best acting part in the historical action of the play; he dazzles us so thoroughly as to disarm criticism. Since this is so, Shakespeare cannot escape responsibility, but in his defense it may be said that he has put up plenty of signposts to show which way our sympathies should take."

123

(e) ". . . by the play's end, Hal casts an inclusive shadow. He has met the claims of Hotspur's world, of Falstaff's, and of Henry's, without narrowing himself to any one. He has practiced mercy as well as justice, politics as well as friendship, shown himself capable of mockery as well as reverence, detachment as well as commitment, and brought into a practicable balance court, field, and tavern."

2. Assess carefully what "honor" means to each of the following, using all the evidence provided by the play and indicating the strengths and weaknesses of each position: (1) Henry, (2) Falstaff, (3) Hotspur, (4) Hal.

3. Discuss the many manifestations of the theme of genuineness *versus* spuriousness in the play, including Henry's title to his throne, Falstaff's to his knighthood, the rebels' grounds for rebellion, the numerous allusions to "counterfeiting," etc. What suggestions does the play offer as to what genuineness is or how it can be won?

4. Write an essay on Shakespeare's characterization of Hal, showing how his full quality is increasingly revealed to us through (a) the persons among whom Shakespeare places him (especially Hotspur, Falstaff, Henry), (b) what he himself says and does, and (c) what others say of him.

QUESTIONS

[*I i*]

One of the main jobs of any play's opening scene is to introduce the audience to some or all of its personages and to some or all of the events, problems, and confrontations in which these personages are or will be involved.

1. Shakespeare's first scene in this play presents only two personages but refers to several more. Where are the following referred to and how much do we learn about each: (a) Mortimer, (b) Glendower, (c) Hotspur, (d) Archibald, Earl of Douglas, (e) Sir Walter Blunt, (f) the Earl of Northumberland, (g) the Earl of Worcester?

2. In 1399, having deposed Richard II by force and then arranged his murder in prison, Henry vowed a Crusade to expiate his guilt. It is now a year later, and he has not fulfilled his vow. What has prevented him? What new events look as if they too might prevent him?

3. At the time of the play, Wales and Scotland were traditional enemies of England, not, as now, parts of a United Kingdom. Why is the news from Wales called "heavy" (37)? What aspect of the total news from Scotland is really "smooth and welcome" (66)? What aspect of it remains worrisome? What other worries does the king have besides political ones?
4. By what means does Shakespeare convey in this scene the sense that Henry is a strong, shrewd, and resourceful king? How is this sense enhanced by the juxtaposition of lines 49-61 with lines 62-75, and of lines 95-98 with line 99?
5. What confrontations to come does the information this scene conveys point to or hint at—i.e. by the scene's end, what expectations has the playwright aroused in us?

[*I ii*]

1. By what lines in scene i has Shakespeare prepared us for scene ii?
2. How would you describe the relationship that exists between Falstaff and Prince Hal? For what reasons is Falstaff's company attractive to Hal? For what reasons is Hal's company attractive to Falstaff? In what respects does the character of the relationship between Poins and Falstaff differ from that between Hal and Falstaff?
3. This scene is full of Elizabethan slang and of wordplay of all kinds including puns. Scene i has little or none of that sort of thing. What would you gather to be Shakespeare's purpose in making this sharp contrast? What other differences do you notice between scenes i and ii in the way the language is arranged or in the kind of language that is used? What sudden and obvious change of manner occurs at line 180? To what change of content and attitude does it correspond?

[*I iii*]

1. By what lines in scene i has this scene been prepared for?
2. The Percys were among Henry's stoutest supporters when he deposed Richard II. Now he knows that one of them at least is hostile to him. Some critics, therefore, hold that his conduct in this scene consciously aims at bringing them to an open break. What support can you find for this theory in Henry's conduct toward Worcester? toward Hotspur? How could you account for Henry's conduct without such a theory?
3. What engaging personal qualities are revealed by Hotspur's first speech to the King (lines 30-70)? Does Shakespeare in-

crease the attractiveness of the speech and of the person it
reveals through its contrast with the speech immediately
before it (23-29)? What *is* the contrast?

4. What qualities in Hotspur begin to emerge after the King's
departure? What is indicated about him by the nature of his
replies at lines 197-201 and 204-11? What is further indicated
about him by the dialogue at lines 212-62?

5. It can be argued that in the dialogue from 146-55 Worcester
and Northumberland are "manipulating" Hotspur—i.e. are
planting seeds of information to which they anticipate he will
react in the way they wish. If so, what are these seeds? What
evidence is there that Hotspur speedily absorbs them? What
reaction do they arouse in him?

6. What clues does the scene contain to the elder Percys' reasons
for turning against Henry? What is Worcester's strategy for
the rebellion? Describe what each of the following is to do to
forward it: (a) Hotspur, (b) Northumberland, (c) Worcester
himself.

7. The farewell speech of each of the three Percys to the other
two is strikingly revealing of his character. How do
Worcester's words reveal him (298-305)? Northumberland's
(306)? Hotspur's (307-8)?

[II i]

1. The inn in this scene is plainly characterized by disorder and
mistrust. The likely inference for a theater audience is that
here is some sort of reflection of England under Henry. What
circumstances show that the inn is physically badly kept?
What circumstances show that the atmosphere is one of mistrust and corruption? How far do both kinds of circumstances
apply to the kingdom?

2. The gist of Gadshill's boasts at 63-83 is that thievery nowa-
days has friends and practitioners in very high places. Of
whom is he thinking? To what other thieves in high places
has the play so far introduced us?

[II ii]

1. In the first part of this scene, what joke by Poins and Hal is
Falstaff the butt of? Would you gather that it irritates him?
or that he enjoys it? or both? Why?

2. Shakespeare makes the robbery scene funny by having Falstaff cry out against the travelers in such terms that it seems
a public service to relieve them of their wealth. List these

terms and sketch the picture they draw of those who are being robbed.

3. On what grounds does Falstaff in line 91 call the Prince and Poins cowards? What is ironical about his doing so at just this point?

[*II iii*]

What does Shakespeare hint about the probable success of the rebel plot through the letter Hotspur receives? In what ways is Hotspur's reaction to it characteristic of him? Why might some of his words remind us of Gadshill at II i 63ff, and what might be Shakespeare's point in inviting such a comparison? What other means does Shakespeare use in this scene to let us into Hotspur's state of mind?

[*II iv*]

For purposes of discussion this scene is best divided into four parts: the episode with Francis (1-105); the episode of the robbery as told by Falstaff and his crew (106-303); the "play extempore" (304-450); conclusion (451-end). The following questions 1-4 pertain respectively to each of these four parts.

1. (a) The joke on Francis is not in itself particularly amusing. The humor of the episode comes from the ancient comic formula of sophisticated jester putting down knuckle-headed stooge. What reason does Hal give for engaging in this little game? What mood and condition is he in that might make this game seem more satisfying to him than to us? What inferences may we draw from Francis's giving him a pennyworth of sugar?

(b) What about Francis's performance at length reminds Hal of Hotspur? What in II iii has prepared us for his comments here on Hotspur? How far are they just? How far are they less than just—i.e. what are *we* aware of in Hotspur that Hal is not?

2. (a) It has been argued by some that Falstaff's language and behavior in this episode show that he enters suspecting who his assailants after the robbery really were and is at first feeling out the truth and then exploiting the advantage this gives him. Pick out the evidence—here and elsewhere in the play—that seems to you to support this argument.

(b) It has been argued that the scene is simply what Hal and Poins anticipated it would be (I ii 168-75): a successful trap which catches Falstaff, inspires him to fantastic lies, and enables them to enjoy "the reproof of this" (I ii 174-75). Pick out the evidence in the scene or in the play that seems to you to support *this* argument.

(c) Regardless which of the above views you accept, why is the joke on Francis an effective lead into this one?

3. (a) In Falstaff's first speech as the King (372-92), he and Shakespeare parody a supposedly "court" style which uses lots of words to say very little and arranges its words in extremely patterned structures of parallelism and antithesis. Point out at least one instance of many words being used to convey very little; at least three examples of striking parallelism of clauses or sentences. By what other comments purporting to come from the King's own mouth does Falstaff make Henry ridiculous? Consider the implications of 376-79 and 388-90.

(b) The hero of Falstaff's performance as the King is Falstaff: "there is a virtuous man whom I have noted in thy company." The villain of Hal's performance as the King is also Falstaff: "that old white-bearded Satan." Is either right? or both? Explain.

(c) What evidence in the speeches of each man as King shows us that under this little spontaneous tavern-play a more serious drama of survival is being enacted by both? What is the relation to that more serious drama of lines 436-49? of lines 416-29 and 450?

4. At the end of the Prince's night of revels, the political world (which has already impinged in the form of Sir John Bracy) is knocking at the door. Show how the scene's conclusion (451-517), without ever explicitly saying so, dramatizes the political world's gradual takeover of the setting, the mood, and the language.

[III i]

1. What disturbing omens for the success of the rebellion does Shakespeare show us here? Sketch the qualities of Glendower as we see them in this scene. Which of them annoy Hotspur? Who behaves better as a statesman, Glendower or Hotspur? Explain.

2. What familiar contrast of attitudes distinguishes the two married couples during the remainder of the scene (191ff)? How does what Hotspur reacts against here resemble what he reacts against earlier in the scene with Glendower? In what ways does the dialogue at 227-44 resemble that in II iii 72-113?

[*III ii*]

1. By what forms of public behavior does Henry say he ingratiated himself with his countrymen before his usurpation? How does he say King Richard's public behavior differed from his? On what grounds does he compare Hal's conduct now to Richard's then? On what grounds does he compare himself as he was at that time to Hotspur now? How far would you say these comparisons are true? and false?
2. Here and there Shakespeare sets up some notable resemblances between the words of Henry in this scene and the words of Hal at I ii 180-202. What are these resemblances? What do you take them to mean?
3. There is an overall irony in the conversation of the King with his son that can be described in the phrase: "The preacher unknowingly preaches his sermon to the already converted." What evidence do we have from II iv that Hal is "already converted"? What elements in the King's interview with his son make it resemble a sermon?
4. Is Henry's response at lines 161-62 in this scene an illustration of Hal's comments at I ii 193-200? Discuss.

[*III iii*]

1. The conversation between Falstaff and Bardolph plays with a number of themes, motifs, and habits of mind and speech that recur throughout the play. Locate all references in this scene to each of the following and at least one earlier reference to each: (a) Being corrupted by the company one keeps; (b) Reform and repentance; (c) Fatness versus thinness as conditions to be valued or disvalued; (d) Children of light versus children of darkness; (e) Quotations from or allusions to the Bible; (f) One further instance that you unearth for yourself.
2. What themes, motifs, or habits of mind and speech that we have met with before come up in the conversation between Falstaff and Mistress Quickly? and in the conversation between Falstaff, Mistress Quickly, and Hal?
3. Compare Hal's final speech in this scene with his final speech in II iv. What differences do you detect and what do they suggest about him?

[*IV i*]

1. Hotspur's response to his father's letter corresponds in considerable part to his response on receiving the earlier anony-

mous letter (II iii). What likenesses do you see and what differences? How does Worcester respond?

2. What two other unpleasing pieces of news does Hotspur receive in this scene?

[*IV ii*]

1. Why are Falstaff's conscripts so ragged and beggarly? What two general groups finally make up his army (see lines 22-28)? How does he justify to Hal their being "such pitiful rascals" (61)?

2. Point out a speech in IV i of which Falstaff's description of his army will certainly remind us. Point out another speech in IV i that we are likely to be reminded of by Falstaff's attitude toward the fate of his men.

[*IV iii*]

1. Sir Walter Blunt's position is plainly that the subject must be loyal to whatever monarch occupies the throne: "anointed majesty" (46). What is the Percy family's position? Is it consistent with their position earlier when Richard was king? Is Henry's position now consistent with the one he adopted then? Discuss.

2. Of what capacity that we have never noticed in him before does Hotspur show some signs by the end of this scene?

[*IV iv*]

1. Where, earlier in the play, was this scene prepared for?

2. What would you say was Shakespeare's purpose in inserting it?

[*V i*]

What does Worcester's account here of the Percy family's grievances against Henry add to Hotspur's in IV iii? Does the King meet his arguments? Why not? In what respect does the Prince's response to the situation outshine both?

[*V ii*]

1. Show why Worcester's argument at lines 5-26 is wholly in character. Which elements in his report of the King's words to Hotspur are true? which are false?

2. Shakespeare has twice put praise of Hal in Vernon's mouth (see IV i 101-14 and here, 53-70). Why?

[*V iii–iv*]

How are certain questions that have been raised by the play
summed up and dramatized in the following episodes: (a)
the confrontation between Sir Walter Blunt dead and Falstaff
living, (b) the confrontation between Falstaff with a bottle
of sack and Hal in search of a weapon, (c) Hal standing over
Hotspur dead and Falstaff playing dead, and (d) Hal finding
Falstaff lugging the dead Hotspur on his back?

SHAKESPEARE AND HIS WORKS

i

William Shakespeare was born in the Warwickshire town of Stratford on April 23, 1564 (a guess based on the record of his baptism dated April 26) and died there on April 23, 1616. He was the eldest of six children of John and Mary (Arden) Shakespeare. His father was a successful glovemaker and trader in Stratford and for a time was active in local civic and political affairs, serving for a term as high bailiff, or chief administrative officer of the town; his mother was the daughter of a prosperous landowner. At age 18 he married Anne Hathaway, a woman some eight years his senior, by whom he had three children, Susanne in 1583, Hamnet and Judith (twins) in 1585.

Although he obviously spent most of his time in London between 1585 and 1611, he kept close ties with his home town, and his own family lived there throughout most of the year. In 1597 he purchased New Place, one of Stratford's finest homes, to which he retired in 1611.

There is no record of his formal schooling, but he undoubtedly attended the Stratford grammar school and got a solid grounding in Latin and literature since the masters during his school age years were Oxford graduates. When or why he went to London and turned to acting and writing plays is not known, but by 1592 he had clearly established a reputation in both fields; and for the next twenty years he turned out an average of almost two plays a year, plus a number of sonnets and several longer poems. He was a charter member of the Lord Chamberlain's Men, an acting company formed in 1594 (renamed the

King's Men in 1603), the foremost company of its time. He remained with the King's Men until his retirement. In 1599 the company moved into the newly built Globe Theater, in which Shakespeare had a financial interest. By that time, and for the rest of his life, he prospered financially through his acting-writing-investing ventures. More important, in his own time he was a widely respected and widely loved dramatist in an age that produced many and for an audience that understood and supported the theater.

ii

A chronological listing of Shakespeare's published works follows. There is no certainty about most of the assigned dates, and probably never will be. As we have indicated in the Textual Note, there was in Shakespeare's day little of the concern we have for the printing of play scripts, and most of the assigned dates for composition are the result of scholarly research and supposition based on both external and internal evidence that we here need only to recognize.

PLAYS

1588–93	*The Comedy of Errors*
1588–94	*Love's Labor's Lost*
1590–91	*2 Henry VI*
1590–91	*3 Henry VI*
1591–92	*1 Henry VI*
1592–93	*Richard III*
1592–94	*Titus Andronicus*
1593–94	*The Taming of the Shrew*
1593–95	*The Two Gentlemen of Verona*
1594–96	*Romeo and Juliet*
1595	*Richard II*
1594–96	*A Midsummer Night's Dream*
1596–97	*King John*
1596–97	*The Merchant of Venice*
1597	*1 Henry IV*
1597–98	*2 Henry IV*
1598–1600	*Much Ado About Nothing*
1598–99	*Henry V*

1599	*Julius Caesar*
1599–1600	*As You Like It*
1599–1600	*Twelfth Night*
1600–1601	*Hamlet*
1597–1601	*The Merry Wives of Windsor*
1601–2	*Troilus and Cressida*
1602–4	*All's Well That Ends Well*
1603–4	*Othello*
1604	*Measure for Measure*
1605–6	*King Lear*
1605–6	*Macbeth*
1606–7	*Antony and Cleopatra*
1605–8	*Timon of Athens*
1607–9	*Coriolanus*
1608–9	*Pericles*
1609–10	*Cymbeline*
1610–11	*The Winter's Tale*
1611	*The Tempest*
1612–13	*Henry VIII*

POEMS

1592	*Venus and Adonis*
1593–94	*The Rape of Lucrece*
1593–1600	*Sonnets*
1600–1601	*The Phoenix and the Turtle*

BOOKS AND RECORDS

Further reading about Shakespeare's times, his theater, and the plays themselves is always valuable and enlightening. Suggested below is a short list of excellent books, most of which are in print in inexpensive editions. Also included is information on available recordings of the complete text of *1 Henry IV.*

Books

(Books marked with an asterisk are available in inexpensive editions.)

* Bentley, Gerald E. *Shakespeare: A Biographical Handbook.* New Haven: Yale University Press.

Campbell, O. J., and Edward G. Quinn. *The Reader's Encyclopedia of Shakespeare.* New York: Thomas Y. Crowell.

Chambers, E. K. *William Shakespeare: A Study of Facts and Problems.* 2 vols. London: Oxford University Press.

* Dean, Leonard F. (ed.). *Shakespeare: Modern Essays in Criticism.* New York: Oxford University Press.

* Harbage, Alfred. *Shakespeare's Audience.* New York: Columbia University Press.

* Kernan, Alvin B. (ed.). *Modern Shakespearean Criticism.* New York: Harcourt Brace Jovanovich, Inc.

* Nagler, A. M. *Shakespeare's Stage.* tr. by Ralph Manheim. New Haven: Yale University Press.

Recordings

(All recordings are released in both monaural and stereo; the text will differ in minor respects from that used in this edition.)

1. Shakespeare Recording Society (Caedmon Records). Harry Andrews, Pamela Brown, Anthony Quayle, Michael Redgrave. 3 12-in. records.
2. The Marlowe Society. 4 12-in. records.